SELECTED
CHESS GAMES
OF
MIKHAIL TAL

Mikhail Tal

SELECTED
CHESS GAMES
OF
MIKHAIL TAL

by
J. HAJTUN

Translated by Róbert Ejuri

DOVER PUBLICATIONS, INC.
NEW YORK

Published in Canada by General Publishing Company, Ltd., 30 Lesmill Road, Don Mills, Toronto, Ontario.

Published in the United Kingdom by Constable and Company, Ltd., 10 Orange Street, London WC 2.

This Dover edition, first published in 1975, is an unabridged and unaltered republication of the work originally published by Sir Isaac Pitman & Sons, Ltd. in 1961 under the title *Selected Games of Mikhail Tal*. It is reprinted by special arrangement with the original publisher.

International Standard Book Number: 0-486-23112-7
Library of Congress Catalog Card Number: 74-83621

Manufactured in the United States of America
Dover Publications, Inc.
180 Varick Street
New York, N. Y. 10014

BIOGRAPHICAL NOTE

Mikhail Tal was born in 1936 in Riga. He learnt chess at an early age, but not too early. His childhood was disturbed by the Second World War, when his parents moved out of German-occupied territory to Iurla, a small village in the Urals. There his father continued in medical practice, returning after the war to Riga.

Little Misha joined the chess club of the Pioneer House of Riga in 1948. He had already learnt the moves from a cousin, but he was twelve years old before starting to learn any theory. His first tutor was the master Koblentz and, as a diligent pupil, he quickly climbed their championship ladder and soon became a first-class player.

The next few years were not particularly successful because he was always meeting stronger and stronger opponents, but stern application helped him through his difficulties. His talent, and particularly his attacking play, began to attract attention, and Shakhmaty S. S. S. R. *mentioned fourteen-year-old Tal as an excellent player.*

He now graduated to open tournaments. In the 1951 Riga Championship he met masters and candidate masters. He had his defeats, but so far from becoming dejected he merely applied himself still more to the study of the game. His next tournament was the U. S. S. R. Junior Championship, and he did not excel here either although he played several excellent games. It was already clear that his talent needed little beyond more study.

Barely two years later he reached the first notable landmark in his rich career by winning the 1953 Latvian Championship and so becoming a candidate master. In this tournament he met all the best players in the Latvian Republic and came ahead even of his teacher, Koblentz, which was promising indeed. Naturally the appearance of the Latvian team, which included Tal, at the 1953 Team Championships of the U. S. S. R. was awaited with some interest. The team gained fourth place and Tal, on second board, scored wins against such masters as Panov and Ilivitsky. Entitled now to play a match for the title of master, he was assigned to meet the master player Saigin. There was a certain piquancy about this pairing since Saigin had beaten Tal in the Team tournament.

Saigin, who was the champion of White Russia, played his match against Tal in Riga in 1954. Tal, who was then a student of Riga University, secured the title of master by winning a fluctuating match 8–6. His outlook on the game was broadening and he emerged as a many-sided player with a primary interest in tactical attacks. But although his play was steadily becoming stronger, he had one marked failing. While finding his way through the most complicated situations, he was apt to make serious errors especially when trying to realise an advantage. This led to severe defeats at the hands of grandmaster Taimanov and international masters Lisitzin and Aronin. In 1955 he qualified for the first time for the final of the U. S. S. R. Championship. In the semi-final at Vilna he came up against the best players of the Baltic Republics, White Russia and the Karelian Republic. He shared 3rd and 4th places with Chukaev behind Kholmov and Nei. It was at this time that the following criticism appeared in Shakhmaty S. S. S. R.: *"Tal is a master of combination and quick to find his way through complications. At times, however, he is too light-hearted and inaccurate in his judgement of position." This was severe but true, and Tal was ready to learn. He had gone far towards remedying the defect by the time of the final in 1956. In this, his most severe test to date, he distinguished himself by sharing 5th to 7th places. Simagin declared afterwards that "Tal is a born chess-player. He almost inevitably finds the strongest line and in double-edged complications his splendid combinative powers assert themselves." It may also be mentioned that a natural optimism enabled him to overcome his defects very quickly.*

His first tournament in the international field was at the Junior World Team Championship in Sweden, where the Soviet team, with Tal on fourth board, went steadily ahead into first place. Tal scored four out of five, and a Yugoslav paper prophetically said: "Tal! Remember this name."

By 1957 as a grandmaster, he won the final of the XXIVth U. S. S. R. Championship ahead of Bronstein and Keres. His play was now described as being marked by powerful energy and a will to win. In fact, he now had chess in his blood, though he was not without other interests since he ended his fifth year at the Faculty of Arts at Riga University with excellent results in history and philology.

In 1958 he won the U. S. S. R. Championship again, the first prize at Portoroz, and obtained the best individual score at the Munich chess Olympics. In 1959 he won the Zurich tournament and the Candidates' tournament, among which personal triumphs a second place in the U. S. S. R. Championship early in the year is rather moderate.

So he qualified to meet Botvinnik for the World Championship and the early summer of 1960 saw the final seal set on a career of unparalleled success.

But before his World Championship match he took part in a small tournament at Riga and had to be content with a very mediocre fourth place. He may have been merely warming up for the main struggle, or possibly he was in honeymoon mood. For just after the Candidates' tournament he had married Sally Landow, a highly talented actress from the Riga Theatre, much to the delight of his mother–his father had died earlier–who regarded the winning of so charming a lady's hand as worth more than the winning of a whole series of first prizes.

Why worry now about the Riga result? Even Capablanca overlooked the loss of a piece at Kissingen when his wife entered the tournament room. The important fact was that Tal settled down to the World Championship match in splendid form. And at last came that unforgettable moment when Mikhail Tal, already the darling of millions and the toast of chess-players everywhere, won the highest prize of all, the World Championship.

CONTENTS

INTRODUCTION

Mikhail Tal, as seen in these pages, is an artist of the chessboard, whose productions are as likely to provoke a storm as win our admiration; but whatever our opinion of him as an artist, we can all glimpse the man himself, driven by his restless inquiring nature into feats of creative activity.

Tal's games of chess, in this selection from his five years of major chess contests, are revealed as true masterpieces, each one bearing his own personal signature. They reveal his imaginative fantasy at work even in the most commonplace of positions and we watch his opponents, however great, transported into a sphere of doubt and uncertainty, as unpleasant to them as it is delightful to the onlooker.

His style is such that opinions necessarily differ, but even the most divergent of his critics agree that he plays "fighting" chess, in which every conception is permeated with white-hot tension. As Ragosin puts it, "Tal doesn't move the pieces by hand; he uses a magic wand." The various elements in his chess make-up are blended into one happy unity; his gifts of imagination and intuition, his speed of thought, his uncommonly retentive memory are all fused together with a quite exceptional daring. If a weak spot is to be found in his play, it is that he is occasionally caught in the whirlpool of his own astonishing imagination; and even then one gets the impression that he still enjoys such rare mischances.

Before proceeding to the outline of his career and to the games themselves, it is interesting to note how some features of this great new chess artist, now World Champion, strike an echo from the historical past.

From the earliest times legends have been woven round the greatest players. In Haroun-al-Rashid's court the ability of the Caliph's younger son to play a game without sight of the board was ascribed to supernatural influences. Even after the Middle Ages such prejudices survived; fantastic stories about the early masters of the modern form of the game were eagerly passed from mouth to mouth and a recurring motif was the "changed piece" and there were other beliefs of a supernatural, even diabolical nature.

Even the nineteenth century produced its legends about famous players, but in the more enlightened atmosphere of those days there were reactions against the myths. The young American, Paul Morphy, when he appeared just one hundred years ago, was, because of his sensational record of victories, supposed to have some strange intangible gift. But after his early retirement his games were examined and analysed in an attempt to reduce him once again to normal proportions; even Max Lange, himself a notable master, tried this with the games of the Anderssen match–and failed. Morphy was decades ahead of his age in strategical maturity and in the richness of his tactical weapons. His contemporaries, suspecting some hidden factor, possibly even mystical in quality, failed to realise that the secret of his power could be found wholly in his actual play.

Later still Lasker's qualities were similarly not recognized universally; one of his chief opponents, no less a first-rank specialist than Dr. Siegbert Tarrasch, even tried to interpret or rather misinterpret the world champion's successes as due to hypnotic influence.

Now, half a century later again, with a new star in the chess sky, a new legend has been born. Around Mikhail Tal, new World Champion, stories are woven which have just as little basis in reality. The truth once again is that there is nothing more than a splendid new talent dressed in a new style, a magnificent artist whose career is already an unsurpassed achievement in this intellectual field.

Chess playing has spread in popularity, especially in the last two decades, and nowhere more than in the Soviet Union. The high level of play there puts the U. S. S. R. Championship among the world's severest competitions. So it is small wonder that Mikhail Tal's victory in the 1957 Championship, when he had been regarded up to then as no more than a talented young master, caused great surprise. Nevertheless his sensational score was considered to be in some degree no more than a freak of tournament luck; while it was recognized that his play was full of invention and that his ideas and surprise attacks, spiced with daring sacrifices, often fatally unsettled his opponents, yet it was felt that others also possessed at least his talent and, though less sensational, were probably sounder and intrinsically stronger.

Then came the Championship of 1958. Again Tal was the winner, picking up his points in games where a maelstrom of complications defied solution. The young grandmaster from Riga became the darling of the public, for he was bold and daring, no matter who his opponent, and his games were both entertaining and exciting. As for the experts, they too praised and extolled him but there was still a sense of reservation in their acknowledgements. Only Keres, the combinative genius of the thirties and himself a favourite with millions of amateurs, fully appreciated Tal's play; in a profound essay he wrote, "Tal enjoys excitement and hair-raising complications and in that kind of game he can find his way around better than anyone else."

Mikhail Tal, twice Soviet champion and international grandmaster, came to the Portoroz international tournament of 1958 with no lack of authority but among the world's best players (only Botvinnik, Keres and Smyslov were absent) he was hardly expected to do more than obtain a distinguished position in the prize list; once more he startled his critics by qualifying for the following year's Candidates' tournament as a clear winner. Successful for the first time outside the Soviet Union, he not only won but came ahead of a leading world championship contender of the recent past in David Bronstein, acknowledged one of the world's best players.

With three great victories in two years, three first prizes in three major tournaments, his genius could no longer be denied. Yet the sceptics remained sceptical about his future. His games were put under the microscope, his combinations examined from every angle; and sure enough, the sceptics found flaws here and there, though their discoveries no more disturbed Tal than they helped his opponents.

A characteristic of Tal's style is complication, a degree of complication so intense that powers of calculation are rendered quite useless and an indefinable "chess sense" becomes the only important factor. This chess sense, important to any tactical player, is possessed by Tal in full measure and, moreover, in him it is developed and refined to a hitherto unknown degree. This accounts for his phenomenal speed of play and explains why he needs to spend only a few minutes over the most complicated positions. In analysis after a game he shows off the variations like a virtuoso; sacrifices, traps and ideas pursue one another with kaleidoscopic rapidity.

Chess is his passion and he brings to it the creativeness of the inventor and a determined will to win. On the morning before an important game his preparation frequently involves some thirty or forty skittle games or the study of some hundreds of variations. Capablanca took his chess equally lightly, equally confidently, but his aim was the simple position and the forced variation; Tal prefers to drag his opponent to the edge of a precipice and he is seldom the one that tumbles over it.

In the autumn of 1958 he attended the Chess Olympics at Munich with a burden of world fame on his shoulders. Playing as a member of the Soviet team he returned the best individual score and arrived home with an Olympic medal as reward.

1959 was to prove a year of newer and greater successes. At the start of the year he only came second behind Petrosian in the U. S. S. R. Championship, but his play was as sparkling as ever. Scarcely a month later he won first prize in the grandmaster tournament at Zurich, though Keres was a competitor; the local press on this occasion nicknamed him "The Black Panther."

With these tournaments as mere preliminaries he went on to the Candidates' tournament. Although a larger section of world opinion now supported him, few were bold enough to forecast before so great a tournament who would come *primus inter pares,* when the field included Smyslov, former world champion and twice a winner at previous Candidates' tournaments, and Keres, the perennial runner-up, both more highly thought of than Tal. Yet if not a favourite, Tal was at least regarded as the best long shot among the outsiders. And as the tournament proceeded, the long shot became first the favourite and finally the winner. Thus Mikhail Tal won the right to challenge for the World Championship title, and his first thought was that, though he had never yet had the opportunity of playing a world champion, he now had a whole match of such games before him.

The meeting of the two masters for the world title split the chess world into two camps—those who staked their faith on Botvinnik and those who were as ardently in favour of the challenger. When Lasker challenged Steinitz, it was a challenge of the younger generation against the older; when Alekhine challenged Capablanca, it was a challenge of the dynamic style against the classical style. Now, as Tal challenged Botvinnik, it was a challenge on both counts, a fight between two generations and a fight between two styles. Botvinnik had three decades of success behind him and to engage him was undoubtedly Tal's stiffest task yet; the grandmaster from Riga fulfilled all the hopes that were pinned on him and, in a match which lasted for 21 games, he emerged the victor by 12½ points to 8½.

Tal's brilliant rise to the summit brought back to life a style of play which the pundits had long since buried among other museum relics. Grandmaster Averbach, who acts as his second, regards him as the apostle of a new style, a psychological-combinative style, rich in mutual chances and aiming to create positions of uncertainty and complications where mere calculation is insufficient. Grandmaster Kotov, on the other hand, will have none of it. He sees Tal's play as no more than the sum of the experiences of his great predecessors, particularly in the tactical field. To him Tal is a bold and energetic player who aims for complications right from the start and chooses openings where his opponent cannot avoid a sharp clash. He admits that Tal has a special gift for judging sharp positions and that perhaps no one else can so surely identify the combinative elements in the most placid positions or stir up a storm so effectively in the calmest waters. When playing against Tal, a thunderbolt may strike from a clear sky at any moment.

Some critics accuse Tal of taking unnecessary risks; others regard the risks as essential to a style which makes chess into a game of hazard. Certainly the risks are there if one calls his daring a risk; at those moments he enters on such complications that the possibility of defeat must be there. Alekhine was once called an adventurer by those who failed to understand his brave experiments and bold openings; and who criticizes Alekhine now?

The weavers of legend have also reared their heads. They have revived Tarrasch's formula and the myth of hypnosis. Did not one of the participants at the Candidates' tournament wear dark glasses to play against Tal? Needless to say, it failed to prevent Tal winning the game and the first prize.

Szabó, analysing Tal's victory in the Candidates' tournament, suggests that we may be entering upon a new era. Unparalleled successes cannot have no effect, nor can it be mere chance that wins five major first prizes in three years. So, like the old alchemists who searched for the philosopher's stone, we should seek some quality in Tal's style or in his will to win which, out of the complications, produces the pure gold.

Other Soviet grandmasters who are known for their bold and aggressive style come in for criticism from Kotov. He pictures them cautiously turning their opponents over, this side and that, looking for a weak spot or an inaccuracy; only if they find it do they attack magnificently; if not, they compromise. Not so Tal. So in the Candidates' tournament, to keep pace with him, his opponents were compelled to play in his style and even Petrosian, likened a few months earlier to Capablanca, had to embark on wild Tal-like combinations. His influence increases steadily. Every lover of beauty in chess now looks to Tal for the profundity and the brilliance he admires, and chess-players everywhere follow Tal's style, or would if they only dared.

No living chess master can claim successes to match Tal's. The meteorlike suddenness of his appearance recalls Morphy, the style of his victories Alekhine. If his secret is to be discovered, then it must be by scientific analysis of his strange, unparalleled genius, and for that we must proceed to the games themselves.

THE XXIIIRD CHAMPIONSHIP OF THE U. S. S. R.

A feature of the finals of the Soviet Championship is that year after year a crop of new talent is discovered and year after year the already large number of Soviet grandmasters is increased. 1956 was just such a year, full of promise in that several talented young masters had won their way through the previous year's semi-finals into this final. Among the newcomers was Mikhail Tal.

The tournament fulfilled expectations with youth well to the fore and Tal himself securing a high place. For him 1956 was his year of great change. Not yet a grandmaster, his results and his play hinted at the genius soon to be revealed in full. His games, and especially the six that follow, show him to be already fully equipped and they rival in quality his finest efforts in the years to come.

GAME 1

It was the XXIIIrd U. S. S. R. Championship which introduced Tal's name to world-wide chess circles; prior to that he was just one among a troop of talented youngsters. The public at once took him to its heart for his refusal to be awed by authority, his willingness to tilt at the strongest grandmasters with his storming attacks. The experts took note too, but only of his tactics. Actually his gifts were already many-sided, and so, paradoxically, we introduce the greatest attacking genius of our age with a game in the positional style. None the less, it is a true Tal creation with its snake lurking in the grass.

SICILIAN DEFENCE

	TAL	LISITZIN
1	P–K4	P–QB4
2	Kt–KB3	P–Q3
3	P–Q4	PxP
4	KtxP	Kt–KB3

5	Kt–QB3	P–KKt3
6	P–B4	Kt–B3
7	KtxKt	PxKt
8	P–K5	Kt–Q2
9	PxP	PxP
10	B–K3	

Lisitzin has chosen a little-played variation which is slightly in White's favour. Any lack of harmony in Black's position is partly compensated by the weakness of White's king's side after 6 P–B4. Because of this weakness Tal plays to castle on the queen's side.

10	...	B–K2
11	Q–B3	P–Q4
12	0–0–0	B–B3
13	B–Q4	0–0

Castling on opposite sides normally suggests mutual attacks on the opposing king. Unsuspected by Lisitzin, Tal is actually playing for a favourable end-game.

14	P–KR4	R–Kt1
15	Q–B2!	

With his previous move Tal engaged Black's attention on the king's side; now he aims at a weakness on the other wing. A co-ordinated attack against two distant parts of the board is a frequent occurrence in Tal's games.

15	...	R–Kt5
16	BxB	KtxB
17	P–R3	

The capture of the pawn on QR7 would be hazardous, for after 17..., Q–Q3; 18 P–KKt3, RxKtP! Black would have a dangerous attack for the sacrifice of the exchange.

17	...	Q–Kt3
18	QxQ	RxQ
19	Kt–R4	

Already casting his eye upon the weak black squares in his opponent's game.

19	...	R–Kt2
20	B–Q3	Kt–R4
21	KR–B1	R–K2

22 P–B5!

A fine sacrifice of a pawn which permits the active co-ordination of the white pieces, spoils Black's pawn skeleton and limits the range of his bishop. Thus there is ample compensation for the material loss, though Black is not bound to accept the offer.

| 22 | ... | PxP? |

An error which allows White to obtain the advantages mentioned above. As a means of meeting the threat of P–KKt4 he would do better either by 22..., Kt–B3; 23 R(Q1)–K1, RxR ch; 24 RxR, R–K1; or by 22..., Kt–Kt6; 23 R(B1)–K1, R(B1)–K1; with equal chances either way. From now on Black plays very passively.

23	R(B1)–K1	R(B1)–K1
24	RxR	RxR
25	K–Q2!	

His remarkable plan begins to materialize! The white K is to proceed by way of the weak squares to the pawns on QR7 and QB6.

| 25 | ... | Kt–Kt6 |
| 26 | K–B3 | P–B5? |

Playing to win the KRP without realizing that then he cannot make use of his K-side pawns to any effect. Better was 26..., Kt–K5 ch; followed by the centralization of his K.

27	K–Q4	B–B4
28	R–Q2	R–K3
29	Kt–B5	R–R3
30	K–K5	

This blend of sacrifice and combination leading to invasion through the opponent's weak squares creates a rare harmony, for which one must go back to the games of Alekhine and Réti to find an analogy.

30	...	BxB
31	PxB	RxP
32	K–Q6	R–R3 ch
33	K–B7	Kt–B4
34	K–Kt7	Kt–Q5
35	R–KB2!	

A necessary precaution against the threat of R–R7. Meanwhile the white king has marched into the hostile camp with the off-hand air of a medieval knight.

35	...	P–R4
36	RxP	Kt–K3
37	R–Kt4 ch	K–B1
38	KxP	KtxKt dis. ch
39	KxKt	R–K3
40	KxP	

The return journey has proved even more profitable. Now it is just a matter of technique.

40	...	R–QKt3
41	P–Kt4	PxP
42	PxP	K–K2
43	K–B5	R–B3
44	R–Q4	R–B4 ch
45	K–Kt6	R–B3 ch
46	K–B7	R–B4
47	R–K4 ch	K–B3
48	K–B6	R–B7
49	P–Kt4	P–R4
50	PxP	K–Kt4
51	P–Kt5	P–B4
52	R–Kt4	P–B5
53	P–Kt6	P–B6
54	P–Kt7	Resigns

GAME 2

Simagin uses an eccentric opening to throw Tal off balance or else to lure him into a rash and premature attack. The outcome destroys his hopes, for genius is not to be thus impeded. A wonderful game results, in which a surprise attack on a solid position and a sparkling series of small combinations all testify to Tal's splendid chess sense.

ANTAL DEFENCE

	TAL	SIMAGIN
1	P–K4	P–QB3
2	P–Q4	P–Q3
3	Kt–QB3	Kt–B3
4	P–B4	Q–Kt3
5	Kt–B3	B–Kt5
6	B–K2	QKt–Q2

If Black imagines his position is sufficiently solid to render any attack difficult of execution, he is soon disillusioned.

7	P–K5	Kt–Q4
8	o–o	KtxKt
9	PxKt	P–K3

He cannot win a pawn by 9 ..., BxKt; 10 BxB, PxP; 11 PxP, KtxP; because of 12 B–R3! with a strong attack already. A nasty little trap!

> 10 Kt–Kt5!

With the obvious intention of sacrificing on KB7, though the soundness of the move is doubtful.

10	...	BxB
11	QxB	P–KR3

12 KtxBP!

Believing it to be unsound, Simagin provokes Tal into making the very sacrifice he was intending.

12	...	KxKt
13	P–B5	PxKP
14	PxP dbl. ch	KxP

15   R–Kt1!

The first point of the combination; Black is to find that he cannot get his king into safety.

15 ...	QxR
16 Q–B4 ch	K–Q3
17 B–R3 ch	K–B2
18 RxQ	BxB

On a material count Black has no cause for complaint, but White's two pieces easily soften up the black position and Black can never get his pieces into co-ordinated action.

19 Q–Kt3	B–K2
20 QxP ch	K–Q3
21 PxP ch	KtxP
22 R–Q1 ch	K–K3
23 Q–Kt3 ch	K–B4
24 R–B1 ch	

Step by step the noose is drawn tighter.

24 ...	K–K5

Looking for shelter in the middle of the board; an interesting idea which is forced upon him since the natural-looking 24 . . . , K–Kt3; would lose material. Nevertheless, as the game shows, he cannot avoid the fatal square.

25 R–K1 ch	K–B4
26 P–Kt4 ch	K–B3
27 R–B1 ch	K–Kt3

28 Q–K6 ch	K–R2

Now we can see why Black tried to avoid the square KKt3; he cannot play 28 . . ., B–B3; on account of 29 Q–B5 ch, K–B2: 30 QxKt.

29 QxKt	KR–K1
30 R–B7!	

The attack persists. Tal goes on combining, almost out of spite, until victory is won.

30 ...	B–B1
31 Q–B5 ch	K–Kt1
32 K–B2	

The safety of his own king must be attended to, and he finds a suitable square on his KR4.

32 ...	B–B4 ch
33 K–Kt3	R–K6 ch
34 K–R4	R(R1)–K1

35   RxP ch!

This second sacrifice of a rook, as surprising as the first, leads to a winning end-game. The sheer beauty of the game is enhanced by the way in which Tal handles pure technicalities with "little combinations."

35 ...	KxR
36 QxB	R(K1)–K3
37 QxP ch!	K–Kt3
38 Q–R8	K–B3

39	P–R4!	K–K4
40	P–R5	K–Q4
41	Q–Q8 ch	K–K5
42	P–R6	K–B6
43	P–R7	R–K7
44	Q–Q3 ch	R(K3)–K6
45	QxR(K3) ch!	Resigns

GAME 3

The splendid ending of this game against Khasin is most memorable. Initiative is the breath of life to Tal and, as here, he is ready to pay a great price for it; the decisive combination occurs in one of those carefully created positions of uncertainty. In the opening Tal does not look for the move which is absolutely best, but contents himself often with the second or third best and in that respect also this game is typical of his style.

SICILIAN DEFENCE

	KHASIN	TAL
1	P–K4	P–QB4
2	Kt–KB3	Kt–QB3
3	P–Q4	PxP
4	KtxP	Kt–B3
5	Kt–QB3	P–Q3
6	B–QB4	P–K3
7	0–0	P–QR3

Preparing for an early advance on the queen's side, though 7 . . . , B–K2; is a more accurate defence.

8   B–K3

8 B–KKt5, is more energetic.

8	. . .	Q–B2
9	B–Kt3	B–K2

Transposing back into the variation he left two moves earlier.

10   P–B4   P–QKt4!?

And at once diverging again, the usual line being 10 . . . , 0–0.

11   P–B5!

The most energetic move, and better than 11 Q–B3. White's position is now slightly the better.

11	. . .	KtxKt
12	QxKt	

If BxKt, Black obtains a free game by 12 . . . , P–Kt5; 13 Kt–K2, P–K4; 14 B–K3, 0–0.

12	. . .	0–0
13	PxP?	

With QR–Q1 White, already having an advantage in space, might well have stepped up the pressure. He could not gain any advantage by 13 P–QR4, because of the reply B–Q2.

13   . . .   BxP

PxP would not do because of the surprising move 14 Kt–Q5!, with advantage to White, as the following variations show:

   I. 14 . . . , KtxKt; 15 BxKt, R–Kt1; 16 RxR ch, BxR; 17 Q–R7!, B–Kt2; 18 BxP ch, K–R1; 19 B–Kt6, and wins.

  II. 14 . . . , PxKt; 15 BxP ch, KtxB; 16 QxKt ch, K–R1; 17 RxR ch, BxR; 18 QxR, and wins.

 III. 14 . . . , Q–Kt2; 15 KtxB ch, QxKt; 16 B–KB4, and 17 QR–Q1.

14	QR–Q1	QR–B1
15	K–R1	

The position is now equal. White's slight advantage in space is offset by Black's counter-chances on the QB file.

15	. . .	KR–Q1
16	Kt–Q5?	

A second faulty plan, which renders the KB inactive because of the weakness of the QBP and the closing of the diagonal. 16 B–Kt5 came much more into consideration.

| 16 | ... | BxKt |
| 17 | PxB | Kt–Q2 |

Now Black has the better game, with all his pieces in active play.

| 18 | Q–KB4 | B–B3 |
| 19 | B–Q4 | R–KI! |

BxB looks attractive, since the reply 20 QxBP ch, would cost White his queen. The text-move earns its exclamation mark because White would actually answer 19 ..., BxB; with 20 RxB, Kt–K4; 21 P–B3, R–KI; 22 B–B2, and so obtain a dangerous attack on the K side.

| 20 | P–B3 | R–K2 |

R–K7 would be a blunder, answered by 21 Q–Kt4!

| 21 | B–QB2 | BxB |
| 22 | Q–R4 | |

An illusory threat, which only advances Black's game. Better was 22 RxB.

22	...	Kt–B1
23	RxB	R–K7
24	B–B5	R(B1)–K1!

Black now seizes a definite initiative and develops a wonderful combination out of it.

| 25 | R–QKt4 | R–Q7 |
| 26 | B–K4 | Q–K2 |

Kt–Kt3 also came into consideration.

| 27 | Q–KI? | |

This leads to the eventual loss of the game. There was more hope in 27 Q–B4, R–K7; 28 Q–B3, because now 28 ..., RxB; fails after 29 RxR, QxR; 30 QxP ch.

| 27 | ... | RxQP! |

The fireworks start with a fine example of a combination based on the pin of a piece.

| 28 | Q–B2 | |

If 28 BxR, Black has the threat 28 ..., QxQ!; 29 BxP ch, K–R1; 30 R–KB4, Kt–Kt3!

| 28 | ... | R–K4 |
| 29 | B–Q3 | |

White is weak on the back rank, while Black's sensitive spot is his KB2; on these factors Tal constructs his decisive combination. A striking feature of his plan is that the knight which has been serving a defensive purpose on his KB1 appears in the middle of White's position in only three more moves.

| 29 | ... | Kt–Q2! |
| 30 | R–KB4 | |

| 30 | ... | Kt–B4! |
| 31 | RxP | |

A move with the bishop would allow the entry of the black rook at his K7.

31	...	KtxB
32	Q–B3	

32	...	R–K8!

And now the brilliant finish! This decisive combination exploits the weakness of the back rank in a surprising fashion.

33	Q–Q5	

If 33 RxQ, Black wins by 33 ..., RxR ch; 34 QxR, RxR; and there is no answer to the threat of R–K8.

33	...	QxR!

A move that deserves another diagram.

34	QxQ ch	K–R1
35	K–Kt1	RxR ch
36	QxR	R–K8

And White resigned in a few more moves.

GAME 4

In this game both contestants carry similar armament. A few years ago Botvinnik described Tolush as the one master in the Soviet Union who above all others based his play on sound reasoning. Similarly Tal's most potent weapon is the ability to orient himself in complicated situations. Tolush is so rarely beaten at his own game of attacks and richly combinative sacrifices that this game is particu-

larly memorable. From start to finish White's every move in this game is played with a view to attack.

SICILIAN DEFENCE

	TAL	TOLUSH
1	P–K4	P–QB4
2	Kt–KB3	P–Q3
3	P–Q4	PxP
4	KtxP	Kt–KB3
5	Kt–QB3	P–QR3
6	B–Kt5	P–K3
7	P–B4	Q–Kt3

Complications start after only seven moves. At every tournament the theoreticians and the players get together and discuss such sharp variations and the opinions on their merits and demerits vary continually as some innovation is made in a fashionable line.

8	Q–Q2!	QxP?

The QKtP has been regarded as poison by every type of master from the classical Tarrasch to the neo-romantic Tartakover. And still it is swallowed by masters who believe they have found an antitoxin in the laboratory of their analysis.

9	R–QKt1	Q–R6
10	P–K5!	PxP
11	PxP	KKt–Q2
12	Kt–K4	

A perfect example of centralized knights in the Nimzovitch manner. Note that every white piece except the king's rook is poised for attack and therefore the exposure of the white king is of no consequence. The black king on the other hand offers a ready target, especially to the knights. Needless to say, the KP is taboo because of the answer 13 Kt–Kt5!

12	...	QxP

Two years later Tolush himself made a remarkable improvement in Black's defensive system by an apparently insignificant interpolation, as follows: 12 ..., P–R3; 13 B–R4, QxP; 14 R–Kt3, Q–R8 ch; 15 K–B2, Q–R5; 16 B–QKt5, PxB; 17 KtxKtP, B–B4 ch!; 18 KtxB, QxB ch; 19 P–Kt3, Q–Q1; 20 Q–Q6, KtxKt; 21 Kt–B7 ch, QxKt; 22 QxQ, QKt–R3; 23 Q–Kt6, KtxR; 24 PxKt, o–o; and Black won. (Korchnoi-Tolush, 1958)

| 13 | R–Kt3 | Q–R8 ch |
| 14 | K–B2 | Q–R5 |

15　B–Kt5!

A beautiful move introducing a whole series of forcing combinations. From now on Tal does not let his opponent get a word in, but continues on his course with the utmost accuracy. There is no better reply than the text-move, although it brings the knight into action, for if 15 ..., Q–R7; 16 Q–B3!

| 15 | ... | PxB |
| 16 | KtxKtP | P–B3 |

Forced by the threat of 17 Kt–B7 mate. If 16 ..., Kt–R3; White can force the issue by 17 Kt(4)–Q6 ch.

| 17 | PxP | PxP? |

A mistake which allows White's attack to gain momentum. KtxP gave much better defensive chances and even QxKt(K5)

with the threat of B–B4 ch came into consideration.

18　R–K1!

One more effect of the initial B-sacrifice is that the only inactive piece now comes to life. The move is far from obvious, but the superficially attractive 18 Kt–B7 ch, is satisfactorily met by K–B2, since the capture of Black's QR would only simplify the position while leaving Black with a material advantage.

| 18 | ... | R–R3 |

Not PxB because of 19 Kt–B7 ch, K–B2; 20 R–B3 ch, or if 19 ..., K–K2; 20 Q–Q6 ch, leading to mate in either case.

19	BxP	KtxB
20	KtxKt ch	K–B2
21	R–KB3!	

A key move in the weaving of a mating net, though the winning process is still far from easy.

| 21 | ... | Q–R5 ch |

QxKt is answered by 22 Kt–Q5 dis. ch, and the attack can easily be forced home. Surprisingly enough after 21 ..., B–B4 ch; the king would be safe on KKt3.

| 22 | K–B1 | P–K4 |
| 23 | Q–Q5 ch | B–K3 |

24 Kt-Q7 dis. ch!

The complications reach their peak. Black can only escape mate by yielding material.

24 ...   K-Kt3

The lesser of two evils. If K-K2; 25 Q-B5 ch, K-Q1 (K-K1; 26 Q-B8 ch); 26 Q-B7 ch.

25 KtxP ch   K-Kt2
26 R-Kt3 ch!   QxR

His resistance collapses. If 26..., K-R3, 27 Kt-B7 ch, BxKt; 28 Q-Q2 ch, K-R4; 29 R-K5 ch, with mate to follow. Naturally if 26..., K-B3; 27 Q-Q8 ch.

27 QxP ch   Kt-Q2
28 PxQ   R-Kt3
29 Q-B7   B-QB4
30 KtxKt   B-B5 ch
31 R-K2

The final position. Tolush, with a lost game, overstepped the time limit.

GAME 5

In this game against Ragosin the road to victory is hedged with anxious moments. Though Tal exerts all his will-power to force the issue from first to last, he meets with stiff resistance. Ragosin's highly unorthodox queen manoeuvres take the game into uncharted waters where navigation is extremely hazardous. Tal's intuition in such circumstances does not betray him, however, and he is able to lead into an instructive and winning end-game. It was Ragosin who a few years later described Tal as seeming to move the pieces with a magic wand, and he certainly does so here from the 47th move onwards. The game, in spite of a certain lack of unity, nevertheless creates a powerful impression.

SLAV DEFENCE

TAL	RAGOSIN
1 P-Q4	P-Q4
2 P-QB4	P-QB3
3 Kt-QB3	Kt-B3
4 Kt-B3	P-KKt3
5 B-B4	

An old variation, reminiscent of the Botvinnik–Levenfisch match. White has the easier game with his steady, sound development, while Black is somewhat cramped.

5 ...	B-Kt2
6 P-K3	Q-R4
7 B-K2	QKt-Q2

Kt-K5 would be inferior because of the continuation 8 Q-B2, B-B4; 9 B-Q3, with a further gain in development to White.

| 8 O-O | Kt-R4!? |

A sharp line, getting rid of the white QB at the cost of weakening his K-side pawns.

9 B-Kt5	P-KR3
10 B-R4	P-KKt4
11 Kt-Q2!	

Recognising that after 11 B–Kt3, KtxB; 12 RPxKt, he cannot exploit the weakness of the black KRP as it will be adequately defended by the bishop. The text virtually forces Black's reply, since 11 . . . , QKt–B3; is answered by 12 B–Kt3.

11	...	PxB
12	BxKt	Kt–B3
13	B–B3	

At the end of the opening exchanges Tal has the better position, but Black's two bishops and open KKt file give him chances.

13	...	O–O
14	Q–B2	PxP

He starts to exploit his chances by yielding the centre in order to get his queen into action.

15	KtxP	Q–KKt4

This was the kind of situation Black envisaged when he embarked on his 8th move.

16	K–R1	B–K3
17	Kt–K5	Q–B4

Changing his plan. He recognises that the KKt file offers no prospects, while an exchange of queens (which Tal rightly avoids) would emphasise the power of his two bishops.

18 P–K4!

He seizes the centre, but the weakness of the pawn structure, demanding as it does defence by pieces, is to cause him some anxiety.

18 . . . Q–R2

The queen is on the attack even in this curious position. 18 . . . , Q–Kt4; would be less good on account of 19 QR–Q1, KR–Q1; 20 B–K2, with the threat of P–B4.

19	Q–R4	Kt–K1
20	Kt–Q3	R–Q1
21	Kt–K2	

Before anything else he must secure the QP.

21	...	Kt–Q3
22	Kt–B5	

The question underlying all this cut and thrust is whether White's centre pawns are weak or strong.

22 . . . B–B5

23 P–K5!

Energetic but forced. With other moves White might get into trouble with his KP.

23	...	P–Kt4
24	QxRP	

He must accept this unimportant pawn in exchange for his QP because 24 Q–Q1?, is answered by Kt–B4!

24	...	Kt–B1
25	Q–B7	BxKt
26	BxB	RxP
27	QxBP	Q–B7

Imposing a dangerous pin on the white knight, the consequences of which Tal has taken into account in working out his counter-attack.

28 B–B3 R–QB5

Overlooking White's fine reply. Better was 28 . . . , BxP; at once with equal chances.

29 P–QKt4!

The saving clause! Black cannot play 29 ...,
RxP; because of 30 QR–B1, followed
by P–K6 with advantage.

29	...	BxP
30	QR–K1	B–Kt2
31	P–QR3	

Consolidating the position of his knight.

| 31 | ... | Kt–Q3? |

As a result of his 28th move Black is strategically lost, so he endeavours to work up
a counter-attack by sacrificing a pawn in
order to move his knight from its passive
position on QB1 to an active situation on
Q5.

| 32 | RxP | Kt–B4 |

| 33 | RxP! |

A risky and unnecessary sacrifice. Correct
was the simple 33 R–K2, Q–B6; 34 Q–Q5,
R–B5; 35 Kt–K4, Q–B5; 36 Q–Q2. Tal probably hoped to exploit his opponent's time
trouble with the sacrifice, expecting Ragosin to prove unable to find the best defence.
It is a piece of typical Tal, designed to retain his initiative.

33	...	RxR
34	B–Q5	Q–K7!
35	R–KKt1	Q–K2
36	Q–KKt6	

More accurate was 36 QxKtP, with three
pawns and an attack for the piece. The

intensifying of the complications by the
text-move is only justified by Black's error
a move later.

| 36 | ... | Q–B3 |
| 37 | Q–R5 | Kt–K2? |

Had Black realised at this point that one
purpose of the rook sacrifice was to secure
a favourable end-game, he would have
played 37 ..., Kt–Q3; holding the QKtP.
This omission leads to the loss of the
game.

38	Kt–Q7!	Q–B4
39	BxR ch	QxB
40	QxKtP!	R–B7

P–R6 came into consideration.

| 41 | Kt–K5 |

Tal's plan of leading to a winning end-game
while still a piece down is quite an
astonishing conception.

41	...	QxP
42	Kt–Kt4	Q–B2
43	Q–Q3	R–Kt7
44	Q–K4	P–R4
45	Kt–K3	R–K7
46	P–Kt5!	

A little combination on the Capablanca
model, designed to cause further simplification.

| 46 | ... | B–R3 |

All unsuspecting, he commits the error of
exchanging the strong bishop for the distant
passed pawns. Better was Kt–B4.

47	Kt–B5!	RxQ
48	KtxB ch	K–Kt2
49	KtxQ	KxKt
50	P–Kt6!	

It is now all a matter of timing. The black
knight cannot hold the white pawns on both
wings.

72	K–R5	K–B3
73	P–Kt4	K–Kt2
74	K–Kt5	K–R2
75	K–B6	K–Kt1
76	K–Kt6	K–R1
77	P–Kt5	K–Kt1
78	K–R6	K–R1
79	P–Kt6	K–Kt1
80	P–Kt7	Resigns

GAME 6

Anatole France once remarked that genius is an uncomfortable bedfellow. Bannik must have felt similarly closeted during this game, and not without reason. His position is threatened by intricate combinations all the way from the 8th move and is finally broken before the end-game can be reached.

RUY LOPEZ

	TAL	BANNIK
1	P–K4	P–K4
2	Kt–KB3	Kt–QB3
3	B–Kt5	P–QR3
4	B–R4	P–Q3
5	P–B3	B–Q2
6	P–Q4	KKt–K2
7	B–Kt3	P–R3
8	Kt–R4!	

A remarkable conception. Since White has the advantage in space, the orthodox process would have been to complete the development by castling and then take the initiative in the centre. Tal, however, diverges with a temporary pawn sacrifice, the consequences of which he has carefully worked out.

8	...	PxP
9	PxP	KtxP

Expecting to relieve any pressure on his KBP by exploiting the position of the undefended white knight.

50	...	Kt–B3
51	P–R3	K–K1
52	R–Q1	Kt–Kt1
53	R–Q5!	

Although White has a won game, the technique is not easy. Black has stopped the Q-side pawns and the way must therefore be cleared for the K-side advance.

53	...	R–K8 ch
54	K–R2	R–QKt8
55	RxP	RxP
56	RxP	K–K2
57	R–QKt4	RxR
58	PxR	Kt–B3
59	P–Kt5	Kt–Q5
60	P–Kt6	K–Q2
61	P–R4	K–B3
62	P–R5	Kt–K3
63	P–R6	Kt–B1
64	K–Kt3	KxP

The black king returns too late.

65	K–B4	K–B2
66	K–B5	K–Q2
67	K–B6	K–K1
68	K–Kt7	K–K2
69	P–R7	KtxP
70	KxKt	K–B3
71	K–R6	K–B4

That Black did not resign here or even earlier must be ascribed to obstinacy.

10	QxKt	Kt–B3
11	BxP ch!?	KxB
12	Q–Q5 ch	B–K3
13	Q–R5 ch	K–Kt1
14	0–0?	

Now Black gains a piece with a favourable position.

| 14 | ... | Kt–K4 |

Hoping to create an effective defence by answering 15 P–KR3, with B–B2; or 15 P–B4, with B–Kt5. But Tal now springs a fresh surprise.

15	Kt–B5!?	P–KKt3
16	Q–R3	PxKt
17	PxP	B–B5
18	P–B4!	Kt–Q2?

A grave mistake. He should play **BxR** and after 19 PxKt, PxP!; White's best chance is to play either 20 Q–QKt3 ch, K–R2; 21 KxB, Q–Q2; or 20 Q–Kt4 ch, B–Kt2; 21 KxB, Q–Q5. In either case Black is the exchange ahead and should win.

| 19 | R–B3 | B–Kt2 |
| 20 | Kt–B3 | Kt–B3 |

Q–B3 would not have put a brake on White's impetus because the answer would have been 21 P–KKt4.

| 21 | B–K3 | P–B4 |

Starting to get his own pawns under way at the wrong moment, since White's attack will move faster. It would have been preferable to prepare for defence with Q–K2 and R–K1.

| 22 | B–B2 | P–Kt4 |

Unsuspecting he moves on to his doom.

23	B–R4	P–Kt5
24	Kt–K4	B–Q4
25	BxKt!	BxB
26	R–K1	B–Q5 ch
27	K–R1	R–KR2
28	R–Kt3 ch	R–Kt2

| 29 | R–Kt6! | |

Black must remove this terrible rook which is threatening RxRP and R–R8 ch. But in so doing he reconstructs Tal's pawn position. The united passed pawns soon prove adequate compensation for the piece.

29	...	RxR
30	PxR	Q–KB1
31	Q–Q7	B–KKt2
32	Kt–Kt3!	

Indirectly defending the BP, since if 32 ..., QxP; 33 Kt–R5. Meanwhile the advance of the pawn is prepared.

32	...	R–Q1
33	Q–Kt4	R–K1
34	R–Q1	BxRP
35	P–B5!	P–B5
36	P–R4	P–Q4
37	R–KB1	B–B3
38	Q–Q1	

The whole Q manoeuvre, comprising this and the next two moves, deserves an exclamation mark. The black king cannot be defended on every side.

38	...	P–Q5
39	Q–R4	B–Kt6
40	Q–B6	Q–K2

In view of the mating threats Black aims at all costs to hold his KB3, but in vain.

41	Kt–R5	R–KB1
42	Q–Q5 ch	K–R1
43	KtxB	

Removing an irreplaceable defender.

43	...	QxKt
44	Q–Kt7	Q–Kt2
45	QxKtP	K–Kt1
46	P–R5	Q–Q2
47	P–B6	Q–Kt5
48	P–B7 ch	K–Kt2
49	Q–B5	Q–R5 ch
50	K–Kt1	Resigns

He has no defence against the twin threats of Q–K5 ch and QxR ch.

THE XXIVTH CHAMPIONSHIP OF THE U. S. S. R.

The XXIVth Championship was a notable landmark in the series of Russian Chess Championships, the expectations which it aroused being surpassed only by the final result. Without exception every participant aimed at playing chess that was both artistic and sporting, and this with players of such quality meant that the tournament produced many fine games including some that can be rightly regarded as true gems of chess play. After this great tournament was over, even Keres declared that he was reminded of his own younger days when he had always been ready to sacrifice pieces for the attack and had tried at all times to obtain sharp positions.

But the XXIVth U. S. S. R. Chess Championship was especially remarkable in that for the first time for many years there was the refreshing spectacle of a mere master securing the palm ahead of the many grandmasters, and needless to say this was none other than Mikhail Tal, at the time a bare twenty years of age. The tournament can thus be regarded not only as adding one more to the number of grandmasters but also as marking the real start of an unparalleled grandmaster career. It proved that Tal's play was not only stronger but also more consistent and confident.

GAME 7

The first tournament at which chess clocks were employed was that in London in 1862 and since then time has managed to spoil many a fine game. Goethe described time as an unfriendly tyrant and certainly the majority of chessplayers are all too aware of this tyrant at their elbow. Tal, however, must be excepted. It was apparent to all during the course of the XXIVth Championship, even if it had not been before, that Tal was playing rapidly, almost too rapidly, while his opponents were being suffocated by shortage of time.

In the following game Aronson found the positions so tense and difficult that like many others he became pressed for time and in fact still had four moves to make when his flag fell, though his position by then was lost anyway.

DUTCH DEFENCE

ARONSON TAL

1	P–Q4	P–K3
2	P–QB4	P–KB4
3	Kt–KB3	Kt–KB3
4	Kt–B3	B–K2
5	P–KKt3	O–O
6	B–Kt2	P–Q3

Employing a loose fan-like pawn structure which permits later counter-chances at the cost of a weak spot on Black's Q4.

7	O–O	Q–K1
8	R–K1	Q–Kt3
9	P–K4	P×P
10	Kt×P	Kt×Kt
11	R×Kt	Kt–B3

A well-known position which had previously occurred in the Euwe–Bronstein game in the

1953 Candidates' Tournament at Zurich. Clearly Black cannot take the rook because of the loss of the queen by 12 Kt–R4. He therefore prepares P–K4 though it is by no means certain that it cannot be played at once without this preparatory move.

12   Q–K2

R–K3 would have delayed P–K4, for if then 12 ..., P–K4; 13 PxP, B–Kt5; 14 PxP, BxP; 15 P–B5, B–K2; 16 P–Kt4, B–B3; 17 B–Kt2, BxB; 18 Q–Kt3 ch, K–R1; 19 QxB, and White is a pawn ahead.

12   ...   B–B3
13   B–Q2

13 B–B4, P–Q4!; appears to give Black good chances.

13   ...   P–K4
14   PxP   PxP

This sharp method of recapturing the pawn involves hazards but serves Tal's hopes of counter-play leading to an attack. It is a typical move of the kind that leads to a Tal victory.

15   B–B3   B–B4

It is quite a striking idea to give up one of the two bishops in so open a position, merely to push a white rook from a strong square to one less in the limelight.

16   Kt–R4   BxKt
17   RxB

So far the antagonists have been merely sparring and at this point. White can be said to have a slight pull owing to his two bishops, while Black has counter-chances on the KB file. These chances, supplemented by a shortage of time on Aronson's clock, prove fully adequate.

17   ...   QR–K1
18   Q–K3   P–KR3

Not yet P–K5 because of 19 R–K1!

19   P–QKt4

In spite of his time trouble Aronson accurately pursues the strategical demands of the position.

19   ...   Q–B3
20   P–Kt5   Kt–Q1
21   B–Q5 ch?

An error. 21 P–B5!, would have left a position with equal chances. And next move he commits a further inaccuracy.

21   ...   K–R1

Much better than K–R2 when 22 B–K4!, would allow White to force advantageous exchanges.

22   P–B4?

He could largely have repaired his previous error by 22 R–K1, but the lure of Black's isolated pawn is too tempting.

22 ...	PxP

A startling surprise, White having only reckoned with 22 ..., P-B3. The combinative situation created by White's last move is immediately used by Tal for his own ends.

23	Q-Q2?

There were more chances with the logical 23 BxQ, though after 23 ..., PxP; 24 RxP ch, B-R2; 25 B-Q4, P-K7; 26 R-K1, White certainly has to reckon with a very strong black KP.

23 ...	Q-Kt3 ch!

A necessary interpolation, to draw the white bishop from the defence of his K1. White cannot answer 24 Q-Q4, because of PxP.

24	B-Q4	Q-Kt3
25	QxP	

If 25 RxP, Kt-K3!

25 ...	K-R2
26 QxP	

Not 26 R-B1, because of B-R6!

26 ...	B-Kt8!

The point of Black's combination. He probes the weakness of White's back rank with a series of mating threats.

27	B-K5	Kt-K3!
28	Q-Q6	Q-B4
29	B-B4	Kt-Kt4

P-Kt4 was undoubtedly a winner, but there is no need to wreck his king's position in order to try and win.

30	Q-Kt4	B-K5

The bishop's work on the rear rank is done. Entry will now be made on the seventh rank.

31	BxB	RxB
32	R-KB1	R-K7
33	Q-Q6	RxQRP

A necessary precaution, for if at once 33 ..., Kt-R6 ch; 34 RxKt, QxR. 35 Q-Q3 ch.

34	Q-Q5	Q-B7
35	P-B5	R-Q1

Avoiding a further trap. 35 ..., R-K1; would have cost him the game after 36 RxP ch.

36	B-Q6	R-K1

At this point Aronson overstepped the time limit. However, the game is completed, for he has no defence against 37 ..., R-K8!

GAME 8

It is naturally pleasant to see a young candidate for the title of Grandmaster get away to an excellent start. Nevertheless there were many threatening moments before this second win was achieved. Taimanov must have felt that victory was already his when he was struck by a bolt from the blue and in one horrible moment the whole course of the game was changed. Similar surprises are not uncommon in Tal's games and he has collected many valuable points in this way.

NIMZO-INDIAN DEFENCE

TAIMANOV TAL

1	P–QB4	Kt–KB3
2	Kt–QB3	P–K3
3	P–Q4	B–Kt5
4	P–K3	P–B4
5	B–Q3	o–o
6	Kt–B3	P–Q4
7	o–o	Kt–B3
8	P–QR3	PxQP

BxKt was safe and leads to equality. After
the text-move White obtains an advantage
in space, exemplified by his control of the
Q file.

9	PxB	PxKt
10	PxBP	Q–B2

Even the exchange of queens will not now
ease Black's plight. For example, 10 . . . .
PxP; 11 BxP, QxQ; 12 RxQ, Kt–K5;
13 B–Kt2 and White's two bishops are all
set to come into action.

11	Q–K2	B–Q2
12	P–K4!	

An excellent move which serves the multiple purposes of opening the Q file, bringing the QB into play, giving White a
strong centre and threatening P–K5. Black's
knights are quite helpless to prevent the invasion down the Q file.

12	. . .	PxKP
13	BxP	KtxB
14	QxKt	P–B3

The only move to infuse any life into Black's
position, and one that is forced in order to
meet the twin threats of Kt–Kt5 and B–B4.

15	R–Q1	KR–Q1
16	B–K3	P–K4

Virtually forced like the preceding P–B3.
Hence Taimanov's lack of suspicion about
Tal's intentions.

17	Q–Q5 ch	K–R1

18	Q–Q6?

The correct continuation was Q–B7, but in
order to avoid the complications resulting
from the reply 18 . . ., P–K5; Taimanov selects the text-move, which merely proves to
be a case jumping out of the frying pan into
the fire.

18	. . .	Q–B1
19	P–Kt5?	

Still unsuspecting, though the threat of a
discovered attack on his queen merited attention.

19	. . .	B–R6!

Black rises like the phoenix from the ashes!
Taimanov is now made to pay a heavy
price for his lack of suspicion. And where

is his queen to go? He has nothing better than the place he chooses.

20	Q–R3	RxR ch
21	RxR	Q–Kt5 !

Tal's diabolical trap is sprung and mate can only be avoided by giving up the undefended rook.

22	Kt–K1	QxR
23	PxB	QxKt ch
24	K–Kt2	Kt–Q5

It is small comfort to White that he comes out only the exchange down, since his king finds himself in a mating net.

25	PxKt	PxP
26	B–B4	

26 B–B1, could be answered by P–Q6!

26	...	Q–K5 ch
27	K–Kt3	

He has little choice, since Q–B3 with exchange of queens would be fatal.

27	...	P–KR4!

The net is closing.

28	Q–Q6	K–R2
29	Q–Q7	R–K1 !
30	P–R4	Q–Kt3 ch
31	K–B3	R–K8 !
	Resigns	

If 32 QxQP; 33 ..., Q–Kt5 mate, while other White moves are decisively met by 33 Q–Q6 ch.

GAME 9

It is somewhat surprising to see Bronstein following a faulty plan after his young opponent has indulged in an indifferent opening, and with the white pieces at that. This is just the sort of thing that has led to talk of hypnotic influences; certainly some gadfly of madness hovers around Tal's opponents in many of his games. Thus the present game turns out to be one of those "psychological-combinative" efforts, where one impetus follows another from the middle game onwards until even the ending is dressed with its own combination.

SLAV DEFENCE

	TAL	BRONSTEIN
1	P–Q4	P–QB3
2	P–QB4	Kt–B3
3	Kt–QB3	P–Q4
4	Kt–B3	P–KKt3
5	PxP	

Simplest, but as a result Tal makes little out of the opening, the middle game in any case being his main interest. A more promising line was 5 P–K3, B–Kt2; 6 B–K2, o–o; 7 o–o with some prospects of initiative on the Q side.

5	...	PxP
6	B–B4	Kt–B3
7	P–K3	B–Kt2
8	B–K2	o–o
9	o–o	

The alternative was 9 P–KR3, in order to preserve his bishop. White however allows his opponent the advantage of the two bishops because of the resulting pawn weakness which he can use as a target.

9	...	Kt–KR4
10	B–K5	P–B3
11	B–Kt3	KtxB
12	RPxKt	

The positions are now approximately equal.

12	...	B–K3
13	Q–Kt3 !	

Initiating an interesting and original plan; the position is to be opened up in spite of the opponent's two bishops. Natural and normal was either 13 R–B1, or 13 Kt–QR4.

13	...	Kt–R4
14	Q–Kt4	B–B2
15	KR–Q1	P–K3

As it turns out, 15 ..., R–Kt1!; at once would have been stronger.

16 P–K4!

The advantage in space is increased for 16 ..., PxP; 17 KtxP, would give White pressure on QB5 and Q6, while an exchange of pawns on Black's Q4 would saddle Black with a weak QP.

16 ... R–Kt1

Impatiently played. There were better prospects of defence by P–QR3 with R–K1 and B–B1 to follow.

17 Q–R3 P–QKt4?

P–QR3 was still necessary, though then after 18 P–Kt4, Kt–B3 (Kt–B5; 19 BxKt): 19 PxP, PxP; 20 P–Kt5, White has a pull. Bronstein intends to create complications with his pawn sacrifice, but it is Tal who owns the more accurate compass.

18 P–QKt4 Kt–B5

19 QxP!

Acceptance of the offer demands careful calculation, since capture of the queen figures among Bronstein's plans.

| 19 | ... | B–K1 |
| 20 | BxKt | R–B2 |

R–R1 would now have won the queen, but at too great a cost after 21 Q–B5, R–B1; 22 BxQP (Q–R7, R–R1; with repetition of moves would have been welcome to Black). RxQ; 23 BxP ch, K–R1; 24 QPxR.

21 Q–R3 KtPxB

Not QPxB; 22 P–Q5!

| 22 | PxP | PxP |
| 23 | Q–Kt2 | P–Kt4? |

Another sign of impatience. The ruin of his king's position helps him not at all and he should rather have aimed for a solid defensive position with 23 ..., R(B2)–Kt2; 24 P–R3, Q–Q3.

24 Q–Q2

Gladly exchanging his QKtP for Black's QP.

24	...	RxP
25	KtxQP	R–Kt1
26	Kt–K3	

Moreover the knight has an eye to the occupation of KB5.

Chairman Romanov inaugurates the Tal *vs* Botvinnik world championship series, with Tal and Botvinnik sitting on his left and international grandmaster Stahlberg second from his right

26	...	R–QB1
27	QR–B1	R(B2)–B2
28	R–B3	B–Kt3
29	R(Q1)–QB1	B–B2
30	P–Q5!	

Threatening to supplement action in the centre with an attack on the king, but Black is alive to this possibility.

30	...	B–B1
31	P–R3	B–B4!

Halting the attack at the cost of a somewhat disadvantageous end-game.

32	RxP!	BxP?

Anticipating that with the exchange of all the rooks his two bishops would compensate for White's extra pawn, but the idea proves to be a decisive mistake and better drawing chances were offered by 32....
BxKt; 33 RxR; RxR; 34 QxB, RxR ch.
35 QxR, QxP.

33	RxR	RxR
34	RxR	QxR
35	Q–Q4	Q–B8 ch
36	K–R2	Q–Kt7
37	Q–K4!	

The K side attack is seen to be still on after all.

37		B–B1
38	Kt–Q4	P–R4

39	Kt(Q4)–B2	Q–Kt2
40	Kt–Q4	Q–Kt7
41	Kt–K6!	

A veritable cavalry charge, which will lead to mate or the gain of a piece. Black's next counter-move is already too late.

41	...	QxP
42	Kt–KB5	P–R5
43	KtxB	PxP ch
44	K–R3	Q–Kt8
45	KxP	KxKt
46	Q–K7 ch	Resigns

For after K–Kt1; 47 Kt–R6 ch, wins a piece.

GAME 10

The psychological-combinative style of play also occurs in this game against Bannik. Tal accumulates threat after threat until Bannik is almost paralysed by the storms which hover over his king. As if spellbound he can only watch helplessly when 27..., KtxP ch; threatens the end.

KING'S INDIAN DEFENCE

	BANNIK	TAL
1	P–Q4	Kt–KB3
2	Kt–KB3	P–KKt3
3	P–KKt3	B–Kt2
4	B–Kt2	o–o
5	o–o	P–Q3
6	P–B4	Kt–B3

QKt–Q2 is the more usual continuation.

7	Kt–B3

Better than 7 P–Q5, after which Black could operate on the Q side by Kt–QR4, followed by Kt–Q2, P–QB4 and P–QKt4.

7	...	P–QR3

B–Kt5 followed by Kt–Q2 comes into consideration here. Tal combines two lines in his preparation for P–QKt4.

8	B–Kt5	R–Kt1
9	R–B1	B–Kt5

Not P–QKt4, which would allow White a passed QRP after 10 PxP, PxP; 11 KtxP, RxKt; 12 RxKt, RxP; 13 R–B2.

10	Q–Q2?

The cause of all his future troubles. He cannot prevent Black's P–K4, so he would have done better by Kt–K1 in conjunction with P–B3 and P–K4. There is nothing to be gained by 10 BxKt, BxB; 11 Kt–Q5, B–Kt 2; because Black can then play P–K3 before P–K4.

10	...	BxKt!

Pinpointing the weakness of White's QP.

11	BxB	Kt–Q2
12	Kt–Q5	

Temporarily holding his QP by a counter-attack on Black's KP.

12	...	R–K1!
13	B–K3	

The retreat has to begin since 13 P–K3?, loses to P–R3.

13	...	P–K4!

White's 10th move comes home to roost. His Q4 is irretrievably lost.

14	PxP	PxP
15	KR–Q1?	

He could hold his Q4 for a little by 15 B–Kt5, P–B3; 16 B–K3, but Black will win it in the end by Kt–B1–K3–Q5.

15	...	Kt–Q5
16	B–Kt2	P–QB3
17	Kt–B3	Q–K2
18	Kt–K4	

There is so little harmony in White's game that any better plan is hard to find.

18	...	Kt–B3
19	KtxKt ch	

19 B–Kt5, looks attractive but after 19 ..., QR–Q1, 20 Q–K3, P–R3; 21 KtxKt ch (not BxP?, Kt–Kt5!; and Black wins a piece), BxKt; 22 BxB, QxB; Black has a favourable end-game.

19	...	BxKt
20	P–KR4	

20 BxKt, PxB; 21 R–B2, would have done a little to ease his game.

20	...	QR–Q1
21	Q–K1	P–KR4
22	B–Q2	

Better and more natural was B–R3, hindering Kt–B4 and P–K5.

22	...	P–K5!

White's pieces have all been driven back to the first two ranks. The positional struggle now becomes livelier.

23	B–R5	R–Kt1
24	B–QB3	KR–Q1
25	R–Q2	

The answer to this is inevitable. Better was 25 P–K3, though after 25 ..., Kt–B6 ch; 26 BxKt, PxB; Black has the advantage.

25	...	P–K6!
26	PxP	

34

White is in equal difficulty after 26 R–Q3, PxP ch; 27 KxP (QxP, KtxP ch;), Q–B4.

| 26 | ... | QxP ch |
| 27 | Q–B2 | |

Hastening the end. K–R2 allowed more resistance. What White did not reckon with was the ensuing knight sacrifice and the temporary queen sacrifice on move 29.

| 27 | ... | KtxP ch! |

A fine combination, after which White's position collapses.

| 28 | RxKt | QxR ch |
| 29 | R–K1 | BxB! |

The point of the previous sacrifice. White is now lost.

30	RxQ	B–Q5
31	R–B2	BxQ ch
32	KxB	K–Kt2
33	P–QKt4	R–Q5
34	P–R4	R(Kt1)–Q1
35	K–K2	R–Q6
36	P–Kt5	

Hoping against hope.

36	...	RPxP
37	RPxP	PxP
38	PxP	R–Kt6
39	BxP	RxQKtP
40	R–B7	R–K1 ch
41	K–B2	R–B4 ch
42	K–Kt1	R–K8 ch
43	K–Kt2	R–K7 ch
44	K–Kt1	R–QKt4
45	K–B1	R–Q7
	Resigns	

GAME 11

Klaman also fell victim to a sudden attack, as Gurgenidze did three rounds later, only less spectacularly. Tal's victories against his young rivals in this tournament seemed easily obtained and in this game there is a sense of natural inevitability in the quick and straightforward development of the attack, even down to the brilliant rook sacrifice at the end.

SICILIAN DEFENCE

	TAL	KLAMAN
1	P–K4	P–QB4
2	Kt–KB3	Kt–QB3
3	P–Q4	PxP
4	KtxP	Kt–B3
5	Kt–QB3	P–Q3
6	B–KKt5	B–Q2

An inaccuracy already, though without serious consequences yet. This experiment, instead of the usual P–K3, is not a happy one.

| 7 | Q–Q2 | |

A surprising choice in preference to the normal BxKt. Although White loses a tempo with his queen, it suits him to have the piece on Q4.

| 7 | ... | KtxKt |
| 8 | QxKt | Q–R4? |

P–K3 was still necessary and would have given Black a satisfactory game.

| 9 | BxKt | KtPxB |
| 10 | O–O–O | R–B1? |

35

A further unsound move. O-O-O would have been better, so as to get the king into safety by K-Kt1 and R-B1.

11	P-B4	R-KKt1
12	P-KKt3	P-K3
13	B-R3	

Intending to build up a strong attack on the black king.

| 13 | ... | Q-QB4 |

Observing the threat of KR-K1 followed by Kt-Q5, when the white queen would be splendidly placed on Q4.

14	Q-Q2	P-Kt4
15	KR-K1	P-Kt5
16	Kt-K2	

White is prudent. Kt-Q5 would not now be good.

| 16 | ... | Q-B5 |
| 17 | K-Kt1 | QxP? |

This rash capture costs him dear. He should finish his development by 17..., B-K2.

| 18 | Kt-Q4 | Q-Kt2 |
| 19 | Q-Q3! | |

This fine and simple move regains the pawn by the threat of Kt-B5. The beautiful harmony of White's play is noteworthy.

19	...	B-K2
20	QxP	R-B1
21	B-Kt4	

Another fine move with the double aim of clearing the way for the KRP and of keeping the black king in the centre by the threat of B-R5. One analysis points out the following dashing variation: 21..., K-Q1; 22 B-R5, B-K1; 23 RxP!, PxR; 24 KtxP ch, K-Q2; 25 KtxR ch, K-Q1; 26 RxP ch!, BxR; 27 Kt-K6 Mate. With such variations in the air, it is easy to see why Tal's opponents sometimes make incomprehensible errors.

| 21 | ... | Q-B2 |
| 22 | K-R1! | |

The wise old man keeps out of danger.

| 22 | ... | P-B4 |

Surrounded by troubles, Black loses patience and allows a most refreshing combination. After 22..., P-R4; there is no forced win for White.

| 23 | BxP! | |

| 23 | ... | PxB |
| 24 | RxB ch! | |

There is nothing to be done against such a move, but the swell of the combination is delightful.

36

24	...	KxR
25	R–K1 ch	K–Q1
26	Q–R4 ch	P–B3
27	Q–R6	Q–R4

Black has to let his rook go, otherwise there is mate on KB3 or KR1.

| 28 | Kt–Kt3! | |

More accurate than QxR ch, which would allow Black a chance by K–B2 and P–Kt6.

| 28 | ... | Q–Q4 |
| 29 | QxR ch | K–B2 |

Black has escaped from mate, but that is his only consolation.

30	QxP	R–K1
31	R–QB1	B–R5
32	Q–Q4	Q–Kt2
33	R–Q1	R–K3
34	Q–B4 ch	Resigns

GAME 12

It is no small honour to win the title of Chess Champion of the U. S. S. R., so young Tal's feelings can well be imagined when with one round to go he found himself standing equal first with Tolush and Bronstein and only half a point ahead of Keres. He had to play for a win at any price in a situation where even the greatest of masters could be excused for failing, even if more favoured by the draw than Tal who had to meet Tolush. They were worthy opponents for the climax of the tournament.

KING'S INDIAN DEFENCE

	TAL	TOLUSH
1	P–QB4	Kt–KB3
2	Kt–QB3	P–KKt3
3	P–K4	P–Q3
4	P–Q4	B–Kt2
5	P–B3	

The King's Indian Defence with its complex variations is ideal for those who revel in difficult problems. In the hands of the Soviet masters the defence has been transformed into a brilliant weapon and this 5 P–B3; variation is one of White's best means of blunting it.

| 5 | ... | P–K4 |
| 6 | KKt–K2 | QKt–Q2 |

White's plan is to castle on the queen's side and attack by P–KKt4 and P–KR4, while Black aims to play P–QB4 at a suitable moment. Stronger than the text, however, is the more usual line 6..., Kt–B3; 7 B–K3 (B–Kt5, o–o; 8 Q–Q2, P–KR3!;), o–o; 8 P–Q5, Kt–K2; 9 Q–Q2. P–B4; 10 PxP e. p., PxP; 11 o–o–o, P –Q4!

7	B–Kt5	P–B3
8	Q–Q2	o–o
9	P–Q5	P–B4?

Certain analysts have condemned this move as a grave strategical error. However, it is part of Black's plan to counter White's K-side attack with an attack on the other wing.

10	P–KKt4	P–QR3
11	Kt–Kt3	R–K1
12	P–KR4	Q–R4

Here Kt–B1 followed by B–Q2 was to be preferred. The text-move is a kind of psychological sortie, but White is not a timorous player. It is no exaggeration to regard such queen moves as a spectacular loss of tempo.

| 13 | B–R6 | Kt–B1 |
| 14 | P–R5! | Q–B2 |

His king's position will need defence after the anticipated PxP, while his QP is not exactly healthy either. The loss of tempo must now be admitted.

| 15 | B–Q3 | P–QKt4 |

Neither strategically nor tactically is there a better line than this counter-attack, which must no longer be delayed. That it fails is a tribute to Tal's cool and superlative handling of the attack.

16 O—O—O

A correct decision. After 16 BPxP, RPxP; 17 KtxP, Q–Kt3; Black would manage to stop White's attack with B–R3.

16 ...   PxBP
17 B–Kt1!

Recognizing that the pawn will obstruct Black. Its capture could only have helped Black, who would then play B–Q2–Kt4.

17 ...   B–R1
18 QR–Kt1   R–Kt1
19 Kt–B5!

A positional sacrifice, made at the critical moment before Black's attack gains momentum, which can hardly be accepted. It is not so much the beauty of the sacrifice itself which is impressive as its timing. Tal's handling of the attack is economical and accurate.

19 ...   Kt(B3)–Q2
20 B–Kt5   B–Kt2

The exchange of the King's Indian bishop can no longer be avoided, for after 20 ..., P–B3; 21 PxP, PxP; 22 Q–R2!, or 21 ...,

PxB; 22 QxP, the weakened king's position is indefensible.

21 KtxB   KxKt
22 B–R6 ch   K–Kt1
23 P–B4!

The start of the final assault, threatening P–B5. After Black's forced reply the way is open for the invasion by the QKt and the KB.

23 ...   PxBP
24 QxP   Q–Q1!

Readily offering the QP in the hope that after 25 QxP, R–Kt3; he will continue Kt–K4 with a stubborn resistance in view. But White is not concerned with such trifles as the win of a mere pawn.

25 PxP   KtxP
26 Q–R2!

Here 26 QxP, would be even more favourable to Black, who could then play Kt(Kt3)–K4 followed by R–Kt3.

26 ...   Kt(Q2)–K4
27 B–B4

The only flaw in the game, but one which, owing to Black's faulty answer, has no serious consequences. White should not have offered to exchange the bishop as Black could well have taken it. After 27 ..., KtxB!; 28 QxPch, K–B1; 29 Q–R6 ch, K–K2; 30 QxKt, K–Q2!; the black king escapes, while White is unable to increase the force of his attack.

27 ...   Kt–B1

Now the attack rolls on without check.

28 Q–R6   Kt(K4)–Kt3

If 28 ..., Q–Kt3; White can even play 29 R–Kt2.

29 B–Kt5   P–B3

30 P-K5!

This central break-through, combined in masterly fashion with the attack on the king's side, proves decisive. Naturally the bishop cannot be captured, though it is by no means obvious that after 30 ..., PxB; 31 BxKt, PxB; 32 Q-R8 ch, K-B2; the quickest win is by 33 R-R7 ch!

| 30 | ... | RxKP |
| 31 | BxKt! | R-Kt2 |

Prolonging the fight without in any way helping to save the game. Neither bishop can be taken because the white queen comes in at R8.

32 Kt-K4!

Thus all the white pieces join in the attack. It is characteristic of Tal that he organizes his actions with great energy and his pieces are directed straight at the most vulnerable spots.

| 32 | ... | BPxB |

He has no choice. 32 ..., RxKt; 33 BxR, PxB; fails to stop the attack and loses the exchange into the bargain.

| 33 | R-B1! | RxKt |

Against 34 Kt-B6 ch!

34 BxR

Winning the exchange after all. The first prize is in sight.

34	...	R-Kt2
35	R-B6	BxP
36	R(R1)-B1	Kt-Q2
37	RxP	Q-K2
38	RxP	K-R1
39	BxP!	

Finishing a great fight with a little firework display.

39	...	Kt-Kt1
40	B-B5 dis. ch	K-Kt1
41	B-K6 ch	BxB
42	RxB	Resigns

GAME 13

This next game is a positive symphony of the chessboard, with instrumentation by Tal. As so often, the introduction is quiet, almost peaceful, but the later crescendo comes as no surprise to anyone who knows the fiery quality of Tal's artistry.

BENONI DEFENCE

GURGENIDZE	TAL
1 P-Q4	Kt-KB3
2 P-QB4	P-B4

This opening, about which so much has been written, and which lends itself to transmutation like gold in the hand of the goldsmith, comes more and more to suit Tal's special style.

3	P-Q5	P-K3
4	Kt-QB3	PxP
5	PxP	P-Q3
6	Kt-B3	

A quiet line. Taimanov–Gligoric, 1957, continued 6 P-K4, P-KKt3; 7 P-B4, B-Kt2; 8 B-Kt5 ch, KKt-Q2; 9 B-Q3, 0-0; 10 Kt-B3, with more of an attack.

6	...	P-KKt3
7	P-K4	

A normal line but more provocative than the positional 7 P-KKt3, B-Kt2; 8 B-Kt2, 0-0; 9 0-0, P-QR3; 10 P-QR4, QKt-Q2; 11 Kt-Q2.

7	...	B-Kt2

Black could now have continued B-Kt5 in order to exchange the knight, but Tal is always reluctant to simplify too early. It is a characteristic of his style that he often has no objection to allowing an opponent to develop his plans, as though the bigger the struggle the greater the possibility of finding some unexpected and splendidly combinative counter.

8	B-K2	0-0
9	0-0	R-K1
10	Kt-Q2	Kt-R3
11	R-K1	

Preparing a further advance of the KP, which never materializes.

11	...	Kt-B2
12	P-QR4	P-Kt3!

Played with commendable restraint. 12 ..., P-QR3; would be met by 13 Q-Kt3, R-Kt1; 14 P-R5, whereupon P-QKt4; fails after 15 PxP e. p., Kt-R1; 16 BxP, RxKtP; 17 B-Kt5, B-Q2; 18 Q-B4, and Black has lost a pawn.

13	Q-B2	Kt-Kt5
14	P-R3?	

A mistake which any player might have made, for who could expect the volcano to erupt so soon when there has not been a single underground rumble to date? Of course if White had foreseen Black's 17th move, or even if he had so much as imagined the possibility, he would have played 14 BxKt, BxB; 15 Kt-B4, with a good positional struggle in prospect. But the conjuror does not reveal the mechanics of his magic, though it is all too simple once it is made manifest.

14	...	KtxBP!
15	KxKt	Q-R5 ch
16	K-B1	

He is already in some danger. 16 P-Kt3, B-Q5 ch; leads to mate.

16	...	B-Q5
17	Kt-Q1	

Suffocation is already setting in, and the eruption is yet to come!

17 ...   QxRP!

A well-known motif, but it is one of the
traits of the true artist that simple things
are made to shine in the most splendid
light.

18 B–B3   Q–R7
19 Kt–K3

There is no longer any satisfactory defence. Even worse would have been 19
Kt–B2, B–R3 ch; 20 B–K2 (Kt–B4, KtxP;
21 PxKt, RxR ch; 22 KxR, Q–Kt8 ch),
Q–R5; 21 Kt–R3, B–B1!; 22 Kt–B3, QxKt!;
23 KtxB, Q–R8 ch; 24 K–B2, Q–R5 ch;
winning easily.

19 ...   P–B4!

Opening up the position and bringing in
the reserves.

20 Kt(Q2)–B4   PxP
21 BxP   B–R3

White's pieces are all so thoroughly pinned
that RxB is a threat.

22 B–B3   R–K4
23 R–R3   QR–K1
24 B–Q2

24 R–Q3, would have allowed the follow-
ing splendid conclusion: 24..., KtxP;
25 RxB, PxR; 26 BxKt ch, RxB; 27 KtxR,
Q–R8 ch; 28 K–B2, QxR ch; 29 K–B3,
R–B1 ch; 30 B–B4, Q–B8 ch; 31 K–Kt3,
BxKt.

24 ...   KtxP

In Morphy's games the similar triumph of
the active piece over his passive opposite
number has equally excited admiration.

25 BxKt ch   RxB
26 K–K2   KBxKt
27 RxB   BxKt ch
    Resigns

GAME 14

An important game, since Keres, one of
the greatest of grandmasters, is not only a
fellow Lithuanian but in his youth played
in the same combinative style as Tal and
has been a great inspiration to the younger
man. It is recognized as most difficult to
beat such an opponent since one is de-
feating one's own ideal. This victory and
the method of winning it gave Tal the
much-needed confidence required at a stage
when he was within reach of the first
prize. The complications of the middle
game, as finely interwoven as the pattern
of a Persian carpet, make an indelible
impression, and the short ending is an elegant pendant.

TARRASCH DEFENCE

	KERES	TAL
1	P–Q4	Kt–KB3
2	P–QB4	P–K3
3	Kt–KB3	P–B4
4	P–K3	

These quiet moves may conceal any number of ideas and hidden tensions. Keres
is as at home as Tal in the atmosphere of
complications and concealed traps, but
years have taught him the art of playing
canny and he hopes his young opponent
will lack the patience for this difficult type
of game.

4 ...   P–Q4

Tal counters with true gamesmanship. The
Tarrasch (including this so-called semi-
Tarrasch) version has long been one of
Keres' favourite defences, and to find it
turned against him is probably an unpleas-
ant surprise.

5 P–QR3?!   PxQP

Forestalling White's intention of QPxP
followed by P–QKt4.

| 6 | KPxP | B–K2 |

A move of the QKt would commit him too much. He prefers to sit on the fence.

| 7 | Kt–B3 | O–O |
| 8 | B–B4 | |

Also sitting on the fence until he can see how best to develop the other bishop. This development on B4 is reminiscent of Morphy, whose spirit indeed seems to haunt the whole game.

| 8 | ... | Kt–B3 |
| 9 | R–B1 | Kt–K5! |

Hindering White's P–B5 and opening up the possibility of attack by P–B4 and P–KKt4. A clash in the centre is now inevitable.

10	B–Q3	KtxKt
11	RxKt	PxP
12	RxP	

After BxP, 12..., B–B3; would be unpleasant.

| 12 | ... | Q–R4 ch |
| 13 | B–Q2 | |

Exchange of queens would only give equality.

| 13 | ... | Q–Q4 |
| 14 | Q–B2 | |

It was later decided that 14 Q–K2, was correct, since here the queen interferes with the free action of the rooks.

14	...	P–B4
15	O–O	B–Q2
16	R–Q1	QR–B1

An important decision. The harmonious co-operation of pieces over the whole area is a characteristic feature of Tal's play. If he had tried 16..., B–K1; 17 R–B3, B–R4; 18 B–QB4, Q–K5; 19 Q–Kt3, or again 16..., R–B3; 17 R–B3, R–Kt3; 18

B–QB4, QxKt; 19 RxQ, KtxP; 20 Q–Q3, KtxR ch; 21 QxKt, B–QB3; 22 QxP, he would in each case only have added grist to White's mill. Even 16..., P–QKt4; 17 R–B3, KtxP; 18 KtxKt, QxKt; 19 B–K3, would only have given White a good initiative.

| 17 | B–K3 | Kt–R4 |

A king's side attack by P–KKt4 would still be premature because of 18 R–B5, Q–Q3 (BxR would involve too great a risk); 19 P–Q5, Kt–K4; 20 KtxKt, QxKt; 21 PxP, and the complications are in White's favour.

18	RxR	RxR
19	Q–K2	B–Q3
20	Kt–K5	

White finds himself in some positional difficulty. For instance, if 20 R–QB1, RxR ch; 21 BxR, Kt–Kt6; 22 B–K3, P–QKt4; and White's game is far from easy.

20	...	B–R5
21	R–K1	BxKt
22	PxB	R–Q1
23	P–QKt4	

B–Kt1 would be answered by B–Q8, while after 23 B–B2, BxB; 24 QxB, Kt–B3; White is equally at fault. Possibly he overlooked Black's reply to the text.

23	...	B–B3
24	P–B3	QxB
25	QxQ	

Probably 25 PxKt, QxP; 26 P–R6, PxP;
27 BxP, was better.

25	...	RxQ
26	PxKt	RxP
27	BxP	RxRP

Black has obtained a winning position,
but the technique is difficult owing to the
bishops of opposite colours.

28	B–Q4	R–R7
29	R–Kt1	R–Q7
30	B–B3	R–QB7
31	B–Q4	K–B2
32	P–R4	

P–R3 was comparatively better, but Black
would still win by 32..., P–B5; 33
R–Kt2, R–B8 ch; 34 K–B2, K–Kt3; with
35..., K–B4; to follow. The text-move
makes the weaknesses in White's game
even more apparent.

32	...	K–Kt3
33	R–Kt4	P–R3
34	R–Kt2	

There is no defence against the penetra-
tion by the black king, but White grasps
the illusory hope that exchange of rooks
will increase his drawing chances.

34	...	RxR
35	BxR	K–R4
36	B–R3	KxP
37	B–B8	K–Kt6
38	BxP	P–R4
39	B–R6	

39	...	BxP

Though Black wins in any case, this effective move, as excellent as it is simple, deserves a diagram to illustrate one more
facet of the virtuoso's play.

40	PxB	KxP
41	K–B1	P–Kt4
42	B–Q2	P–R5
43	B–Kt4	P–R6
44	K–Kt1	K–Kt6
	Resigns	

THE XXVTH CHAMPIONSHIP OF THE U. S. S. R.

Every third year, when the International Chess Federation (F. I. D. E.) holds its Zonal tournaments in preparation for the next World Championship, it treats the Soviet Union as one of the zones. Thus every third U. S. S. R. Championship is at the same time a Zonal tournament and it is a special mark of honour that the first four qualify for the Interzonals. That the XXVth Championship was also a Zonal tournament partly accounts for its having an exceptionally strong entry, including no less than eleven international grandmasters. A whole group of competitors were neck and neck throughout and only the final round clarified the position; Mikhail Tal was champion once again!

The field for the XXVth U. S. S. R. Championship was as strong as that for a Candidates' Tournament. In spite of the absence of Botvinnik and Smyslov, who were engaged in their World Championship match, and of Keres, the competitors still included such names as Bronstein, Spassky, Petrosian, Taimanov, Averbach, Boleslavsky, Geller, Korchnoi, Kotov and Tolush. This meant that including Tal there were eleven grandmasters playing and in such a field it would have been exceptional for the defending champion to retain his title. Tal was the exceptional exception.

After the tournament Bronstein wrote this about Tal's achievement: "Mikhail Tal's achievement in repeating his victory of the previous year is all the greater for his having only competed three time in all. His faculty for quick and deep calculation, his ability to guide the play into lines to his own taste and to raise complications in what are apparently the quietest of positions is only matched by his ability to discern and defeat his opponent's combinative plans. He is remarkably successful and had a greater number of wins than any other competitor; some were aided by luck, but fortune favours the brave. Tal is seldom short of time, so naturally he is regarded unofficially as the champion of lightning chess in the Soviet Union. He took part *hors concours* in the Moscow Lightning Chess Championship and won first place ahead of Spassky and Petrosian. His only defect is that he seeks a violent solution even when a patient positional accumulation of advantages would be preferable. When he comes to play in international tournaments for the World Championship he may at last rid himself of this fault and so become one of the most formidable of all contestants."

Time very soon justified Bronstein's forecast.

GAME 15

Tal's first-round win against Tolush reveals the many-sidedness of his play. He exploits a small opening inaccuracy by Tolush in classic style and is not averse to a number of exchanges in the process. Significantly these exchanges do nothing to lessen the tension; with his 19th move he asserts the superior co-ordination of his forces and by the 25th is in a position to force a problem-like finish.

NIMZO-INDIAN DEFENCE

	TAL	TOLUSH
1	P–Q4	Kt–KB3
2	P–QB4	P–K3
3	Kt–QB3	B–Kt5
4	P–K3	P–B4
5	Kt–B3	P–Q4
6	B–Q3	O–O
7	O–O	QKt–Q2

This move causes difficulties for Black. It should be preceded by 7 . . . , PxBP.

8	P–QR3	PxQP

After 8 . . . , PxBP; 9 PxB, PxQP; 10 BxP ch, KxB; 11 QxP, White has the best of it (Koblentz–Barshankas, Tallin, 1958). Even after 8 . . . , BxKt; 9 PxB, PxBP; 10 BxP, Q–B2; 11 Q–B2, P–K4; 12 P–K4, P–QKt3; 13 B–KKt5, B–Kt2; 14 P–Q5, White has more of the play.

9	QKtxP!	PxKt
10	PxB	PxBP
11	BxP	Kt–Kt3
12	B–Kt3	PxP
13	BxP	Kt(Kt3)–Q4

Up to this point the game has followed a known path, but this move of Black's, intending to strengthen his centre by P–QKt3 and B–Kt2, is new. A game Furman–Gipslis at Riga, 1955, continued 13 . . . , Kt(B3)–Q4; 14 B–B5, R–K1; 15 R–K1, B–K3; 16 Kt–Q4, with a clear positional plus for White. At Hastings, 1955–56, Darga played 13 . . . , B–K3; against Korchnoi so as to lead into an end-game, but after 14 BxB, PxB; 15 QxQ, KRxQ; 16 RxP!, RxR; 17 BxKt, R(Q1)–R1; 18 BxR, RxB; White had an advantage, even though there were technical difficulties in exploiting it. Since the text-move also turns in White's favour, the whole defensive system based on 7 . . . , QKt–Q2; must be highly suspect.

14	B–B5	R–K1
15	R–K1	RxR ch

16	QxR	P–QKt3
17	B–Q4	

The bishop is unusually strong here.

17	. . .	B–Kt2

B–B4 would have allowed for the defence of the KBP.

18	R–Q1	Q–K1

19	B–K5	

Black probably failed to appreciate the force of this reply which still further hamstrings his forces.

19	. . .	Q–Kt4

He could not take the QKtP at once because of 19 . . . , KtxP; 20 QxKt, BxKt; 21 R–K1, B–Kt2; 22 BxKt, Q–B3; 23 BxP ch!, K–R1; 24 BxP ch!, KxB; 25 B–Q5!!, QxB; 26 R–K7 ch, with an overwhelming attack. Nor does 19 . . . , R–Q1; help because of 20 Q–Q2, R–Q2; 21 B–R4.

20	QBxKt	PxB?

A more natural and better continuation would have been KtxB; 21 Q–K7, B–Q4; 22 BxB, KtxB; 23 Q–Kt7 (if Q–K4, R–QB1!), R–Q1; 24 P–R4, though White still has an advantage owing to the pin on the black knight.

21	Q–K4	QxP

R–K1 fails against 22 **RxKt**.

22	Kt–Q4	P–B4
23	Q–K5!	Kt–K2
24	Q–B6	B–Q4

A move which is disproved by a problem-like, if not very complicated, combination. The position was in any event untenable, for if 24 . . . , R–KB1; then 25 P–R3, B–Q4; 26 R–Q3, BxB; 27 R–Kt3 ch!, Kt–Kt3; 28 KtxP.

25	Kt–B6!	QxB

If BxKt; then simply 26 QxP ch, K–R1; 27 Q–B6 mate.

26	KtxKt ch	K–B1
27	R–K1	B–K3
28	KtxP	Resigns

GAME 16

This next game occurred in the fourth round and was another typical Tal effort. Where Capablanca made his combinations artistically and Alekhine dynamically, Tal can be said to make them viciously. White here has no inkling of danger when a knight sacrifice hits him as early as the 12th move. This first attack is followed by a second, even more energetic, wave and the final mating threat is conjured up with even less material than in the previous game.

BENONI DEFENCE

	AVERBACH	TAL
1	P–Q4	Kt–KB3
2	P–QB4	P–K3
3	Kt–QB3	P–B4
4	P–Q5	PxP
5	PxP	P–Q3

In this opening the standard themes are a central attack by White and a queen's side attack by Black, supported by the bishop on KKt2. Tal extends Black's scope by an early and successful attack against White's centre.

6	P–K4	P–KKt3
7	B–K2	B–Kt2
8	Kt–B3	O–O
9	O–O	R–K1!

Working up an attack out of limited resources, though the subsequent developments on White's K4 could hardly have been foreseen at this stage. In a game Smyslov–Filip, Vienna, 1957, Black played 9 . . . , B–Kt5; 10 P–KR3, BxKt; 11 BxB, P–QR3?; with advantage to White, though 11 . . . , QKt–Q2; was preferable.

10	Q–B2	Kt–R3!
11	B–KB4?	

Knowing what follows, it can be seen that P–QR3 was to be preferred, but Averbach had no idea that he was in danger of having a piece sacrificed against him.

11	. . .	Kt–QKt5
12	Q–Kt1	KtxKP!

This move deserves an exclamation mark, for the sacrifice yields a draw at least besides creating the complications in which Tal revels. The move may well be intrinsically the best, for after 12 . . . , Kt–R4; 13 B–KKt5, P–B3; 14 B–K3, P–B4; 15

46

P-QR3, PxP; 16 PxKt, PxKt; 17 KBxP,
PxP; 18 Kt-K4, White has the better game.

13	KtxKt	B-B4
14	Kt(B3)-Q2	KtxQP
15	BxP?	

The losing move. B-Kt3 was necessary,
when the best play on both sides gives
equal chances as follows: 15 ..., Q-K2;
16 B-Kt5, BxKt; 17 KtxB, QxKt; 18 BxR,
QxB; 19 BxP, Q-B3; 20 B-Kt3, P-B5;
with a pawn for the exchange.

| 15 | ... | Kt-B3! |

Recovering his piece with the better game.
Thus the complications have served their
turn once more.

| 16 | B-B3 |

Even worse was 16 BxP, KtxKt; 17 KtxKt,
BxKt; 18 Q-Q1, Q-Kt4.

16	...	KtxKt
17	KtxKt	BxKt
18	BxB	QxB

White is quite lost, being a pawn down
and unable to prevent the powerful estab-
lishment of the black bishop on his Q4.
The fact that there are bishops of opposite
colours does, however, create technical
difficulties, and for that reason Tal avoids
simplification and prepares a direct king's
side attack.

19	Q-B2	R-K2
20	B-B3	QR-K1
21	QR-Q1	B-Q5
22	P-QR4	P-Kt3
23	P-QKt3	R-K4
24	R-Q2	

Aiming to ease his position by an exchange of rooks which Black cannot avoid,
for now 24 ..., Q-K3; is answered by 25
Q-B4, and 24 ..., Q-K2; by 25 B-B6.

24	...	P-KR4
25	R-K2	RxR
26	BxR	

| 26 | ... | P-R5! |

Injecting this stage of the game with
venom also.

| 27 | K-R1 | Q-B5! |

Staggering as it may seem, White must now guard against the threat of B-K4. He cannot play 28 B-B4, because of 28 .... B-K4; 29 QxP ch, K-B1; and he cannot save both his king and his queen.

| 28 | P-Kt3 | Q-B3 |
| 29 | Q-Q1 | R-Q1 |

The rook is going to have greater value on the Q file. *

| 30 | B-Kt4 | BxP! |
| 31 | Q-K2 | |

| 31 | ... | R-Q7! |

A most elegant conclusion to Tal's combination. Naturally if 32 QxR, Q-B3 ch. One cannot but admire the conception and construction of this situation.

32	Q-K8 ch	K-Kt2
33	PxP	Q-Q5
34	B-R3	Q-Q6
35	B-Kt2	

White could have tried 35 Q-K5 ch, K-R2; 36 Q-B4, in the hope of 36 ..., QxB?; 37 QxP ch, K-R3; 38 Q-B8 ch, K-R4; 39 Q-R8 ch, K-Kt5; 40 Q-B8 ch, with perpetual check. However, Tal would still have won by 36 ..., Q-Q4 ch; 37 B-Kt2, QxB ch; 38 KxQ, B-K6 dis. ch; 39 K-R1, BxQ; 40 RxB, K-Kt2.

| 35 | ... | R-Q8! |
| Resigns. | | |

For after 36 Q-Kt5, RxR ch; 37 BxR, Q-K5 ch; 38 B-Kt2, QxKRP; and wins.

GAME 17

It can be as exhilarating to meet Tal the positional player as to meet Tal the tactician. In the following game his opponent chooses an unusual 4th move which creates a queen's side pawn weakness; this seems of little consequence and could probably have been borne. Tal, however, gives an exemplary demonstration of a regrouping of forces to emphasise the weakness after White's 20th move and in the end there is the usual little combination, this time designed to win material.

SICILIAN DEFENCE

GURGENIDZE TAL

1	P-K4	P-QB4
2	Kt-KB3	P-Q3
3	B-Kt5 ch	B-Q2
4	P-QR4	

The usual lines are 4 BxB ch, and 4 Q-K2. The disadvantage of the text is that it does nothing to advance development and loosens the pawn structure on the queen's

Botvinnik and Tal on the stage of the Pushkin Theatre, Moscow

side. It would only serve a good purpose if Black were to exchange bishops.

4	...	Kt–QB3
5	o–o	Kt–B3
6	R–K1	P–KKt3
7	P–B3	B–-Kt2
8	P–Q4	PxP
9	KtxP	

Since the basic idea of the variations in which White plays B–QKt5 is to establish a strong centre, PxP would have been more logical.

9	...	o–o
10	Kt–R3	R–B1
11	B–Kt5	P–QR3
12	KBxKt	KKtPxB!

Reinforcing the centre and opening the QKt file, which is temporarily better suited than the QB file for a queen's side initiative.

13	Kt–B4	P–Q4
14	BxKt	

Since Black's KB plays an important role in the subsequent combination, it might have been better to retain this bishop with which to counter it. On the other hand there was then the possibility of the black knight becoming dangerous.

14	...	BxB
15	PxP	PxP

The consequences of Black's having both the QKt and QB files open for attack will soon become evident.

16	Kt–K5	Q–B2
17	P–KB4	R–Kt1!
18	Q–Q2	R–Kt3
19	R–K3	P–QR4

Since Black now has obvious targets of attack, while White can find little to shoot at, it is comprehensible that White decides to play for a passed QKtP at the cost of a weakness on his QB3.

20	P–QKt4

20	...	R–B1

At once turning his attention to White's QB3 and starting a regrouping of his pieces which only ends four moves later.

21	P–Kt5	B–K1
22	QR–K1	Q–Q3!
23	Q–Q1	R–Kt2!
24	Q–B3	R(Kt2)–B2
25	Kt–Kt4	

In time trouble he overlooks Black's 26th move. Necessary was 25 K–R1, so as to counter Black's Q-side pressure with action on the K-side.

25	...	B–Kt2
26	P–B5?	

Overlooking the following obvious combination, which he could prevent by Kt–K5, though then Black could have continued with 26..., P–K3; 27 Kt(K5)–B6, BxKt; 28 KtxKt, Q–R6; with good prospects.

26	...	RxP
27	P–B6	RxR
28	QxR	BxBP
29	KtxB ch	QxKt
30	Kt–B3	P–K3

Tal, two pawns ahead with two passed centre pawns, has little anxiety about the rest of the game.

31	ʼR–QB1	Q–Q1
32	RxR	QxR
33	Q–Q2	Q–Q1
34	P–R4	P–B3
35	Kt–Q4	Q–Kt3
36	K–B1	P–K4
37	Kt–B3	P–Q5
38	Q–QB2	B–B2
39	P–R5	K–B1
40	Q–B8 ch	K–K2!
41	Kt–Q2	PxP
42	Kt–K4	B–Q4
43	Kt–Kt3	B–K3
44	Q–KR8	Q–B4!
45	QxRP ch	K–Q1
46	Q–R8 ch	K–Q2!
47	Q–Kt7 ch	

After 47 QxBP, would come 47 ..., Q–B8 ch; and 48 ..., Q–K6 ch.

47	...	K–B1
48	Q–R8 ch	K–Kt2
49	Q–Kt7 ch	Q–B2!
50	QxQ ch	

Tantamount to resignation, but there was no defence.

50	...	KxQ
51	KtxP	P–B4
52	Kt–Kt7	B–B5 ch
53	K–K1	P–B5
54	Kt–K8 ch	K–Q2
55	P–Kt6	B–R3
56	Kt–B6 ch	K–K3
57	Kt–K4	K–Q4
58	Kt–B6 ch	K–B4

White here sealed 59 Kt–Q7 ch, but resigned without resuming.

GAME 18

Kotov is himself a fine attacking player and will be remembered for the excellent combinative ability displayed in the Candidates' tournament at Budapest in 1950, especially in his win against Keres. In the following game played in the tenth round he employs his favourite P–KKt3 variation against Tal's King's Indian Defence. He is a great specialist in this variation and has enriched it with many new ideas for White. Here he experiments with a new 14th move, which allows Tal a dangerous and, as it turns out, a winning initiative.

KING'S INDIAN DEFENCE

	KOTOV	TAL
1	P–QB4	Kt–KB3
2	Kt–KB3	P–KKt3
3	P–Q4	B–Kt2
4	P–KKt3	0–0
5	B–Kt2	P–Q3
6	0–0	QKt–Q2
7	Kt–B3	P–K4
8	P–K4	P–B3
9	P–KR3	Q–R4
10	R–K1	

Many moves have been tried in this position. 10 B–K3, was used in the games Dsieviolovsky–Geller, Salzbrunn, 1957, and Guimard–Boleslavsky, Argentina–U. S. S. R. match, 1954; 10 P–Q5, in the game Clarke–Szabó, Wageningen, 1957; and 10 Q–B2, in the game Gligoric–Szabó, Budapest, 1957. The text-move was a suggestion of Geller's, who envisaged defending the QBP by B–B1 if necessary. Of all these moves those by the queen and rook seem the most promising.

10	...	R–K1
11	P–R3	

Worth considering also was 11 R–Kt1.

11	. . .	PxP
12	KtxP	Kt-K4
13	B-B1	P-QR3
14	B-Q2?	

An unhappy novelty, as Black shows. Logical was 14 P-QKt4, followed either by 14..., Q-Kt3; 15 B-K3, or 14..., Q-B2 (or Q-Q1); 15 P-B4, with sharp play for both sides.

| 14 | . . . | Q-Kt3 |
| 15 | B-K3 | |

| 15 | . . . | P-B4! |

Immediately seizing the chance of taking the initiative, since White is in no position to exploit the weakness of his Q4. The knight is forced to retreat to an unfavourable square with loss of tempo, since if it moves to QB2, 16..., QxKtP; is possible (it has been taboo so far because of the answer Kt-R4 trapping the queen), and if the knight goes to K2, Black can play 16..., Kt-B6 ch.

16	Kt-Kt3	B-K3
17	Kt-Q2	Kt-B3!
18	P-QKt4	

With his last move White made a vigorous attempt to recover the initiative and was threatening 19 Kt-R4. His weakness on the long diagonal, however, allows Tal this energetic response. Now if 19 Kt-R4, Black secures a strong square on his Q5

with 19..., KtxB; unless White prefers a grave weakness on KKt3 after 20 PxKt. It should be noted that White cannot continue 20 KtxQ, KtxQ; 21 KtxR, BxR; since Black comes out a piece ahead.

18	. . .	Kt-Kt5!
19	PxKt	BxKt
20	R-B1	B-Kt2
21	Kt-Kt3	QR-Q1
22	Kt-Q2	Q-B2
23	R-Kt1	Kt-K4
24	B-K2	

| 24 | . . . | P-QKt4!? |

For the first time in the game Tal makes a move to create complications.

| 25 | PxKtP | RPxP |
| 26 | BxKtP | |

White could have won a pawn by 26 PxP, PxP; 27 RxP, but Black's counter-chances would make the outcome doubtful. Kotov plays more prudently and in doing so finds he has taken the greater risk.

26	...	BxP
27	B-K2	Q-Q2
28	BxB	KtxB
29	K-Kt2	P-R4
30	B-Kt5	

30	...	B-Q5!

A typical Tal move. The sacrifice of the exchange is sound in that Black can draw by perpetual check. Alternatively he has the option of trying for more by 31 BxR, KtxP; 32 Q-Kt3 (probably best), Q-R6 ch; 33 K-B3, RxB; 34 K-K2, P-Q4; and White's king still cannot reach a safe haven. Whichever way Black might have chosen to play it, White should now have accepted the sacrifice; by refusing it he loses.

31	R-K2	P-B3
32	B-B4	P-Kt4
33	P-B3	Kt-B7
34	RxKt	BxR
35	KxB	PxB

And so it is Black who is the exchange ahead, an advantage which he turns to account by accurate play.

36	PxKBP	Q-QR2!
37	Q-Kt3 ch	

Aiming by an exchange of queens to ease the attacks on his insecure K.

37	...	P-B5 dis. ch
38	Q-K3	QxQ ch
39	KxQ	P-Q4
40	R-Kt1 ch	K-B2
41	K-K2	P-B6
42	Kt-Kt3	PxP
43	R-QB1	

Or 43 PxP, R-KKt1!

43	...	PxP dbl. ch
44	KxP	R-Q6 ch
45	K-B2	P-B7
46	Kt-B5	R-Q7 ch
47	K-B3	

47	...	R-K8!
48	RxR	R-Q8
	Resigns	

GAME 19

Tal's struggle against Taimanov was even greater than in the previous year. Taimanov did not handle the opening accurately and Tal obtained excellent attacking chances by a fine temporary pawn sacrifice. However, failing to develop his chances with his customary energy, he allowed Taimanov to exchange queens and only a serious error later gave him a whole point.

SICILIAN DEFENCE

TAL	TAIMANOV
1 P–K4	P–QB4
2 Kt–KB3	P–K3

This move, in conjunction with P–QR3, has been repeatedly played in recent tournaments. It is a revival of the old Paulsen defence in an improved form. Soviet masters have introduced several new ideas for both sides into the variation and while its merits have not yet been strictly determined, it is at least regarded as viable.

3 Kt–B3

Black can now equalize easily. 3 P–Q4, PxP; 4 KtxP, gives more chances and after 4 . . . , P–QR3; 5 P–QB4, with complicated lines, or else this knight can at last be developed satisfactorily on the 5th move.

3 . . .	P–QR3
4 P–KKt3	P–QKt4
5 P–Q4	PxP
6 KtxQP	B–Kt2

The best way to equalize was 6 . . . , P–Kt5; and only then 7 . . . , B–Kt2.

7 B–Kt2	Kt–KB3
8 o–o	B–Kt5

After this White develops a dangerous attack. Safer was 8 . . . , P–Kt5; for although White has an initiative after 9 Kt–Q5, PxKt; 10 PxP, a forced continuation cannot be seen.

9 P–K5!	BxB
10 KxB	BxKt

A necessary exchange because of the threat of Kt–K4, but his king's wing is decidedly weakened by it.

11 PxB	Kt–Q4
12 Q–Kt4	

Much better than Kt–B5. Now Black cannot castle, while 12 . . . , P–Kt3; would leave him very weak on the black squares.

12 . . .	K–B1
13 P–KB4	

He is over-anxious to open the KB file. P–QR4 was a strong preliminary.

13 . . .	P–KR4
14 Q–B3	Kt–QB3

He cannot prevent the break-through by P–B5, so he indirectly defends his KB2 by exchanging the centralized knight.

15 P–B5	KtxKt
16 PxKt	Q–B2

17 P–B4!

A very fine temporary pawn sacrifice! Capture by the queen is impossible since the queen is tied to the second rank in order to defend KB2 after PxKP, QPxP. So capture by the pawn is forced and the next four moves reveal that the pawn is untenable and the QB file will be opened.

17 . . .	PxP
18 B–R3 ch	K–Kt1
19 B–Q6	Q–R2
20 B–B5!	Q–B2
21 QR–B1	Q–B3

21 . . . , P–B6; would allow 22 RxP!, KtxR; 23 QxR ch, K–R2; 24 Q–B3, Kt–Q4; 25 PxP, with great advantage to White.

22 K–Kt1

If 22 RxP?, then Kt–K6 ch wins. Nor is 22 PxP, any help since QxP holds the square KB2.

22 ...   PxP

Otherwise White gets good tactical chances, but now his Q4 is weak.

23 RxP   R–QB1

24 R(B1)–B1

An obvious move but not the strongest, since Black can now defend himself by an exchange of queens. Tal could have put more difficulties in Black's way by 24 R(B4)–B1, with the threat of 25 B–R3, and after 24..., Q–K3 (to defend KB2); 25 B–Q6!, RxR; 26 RxR, P–Kt3; 27 R–B5!, when White must win.

24 ...   Kt–Kt3!
25 QxQ   RxQ
26 R–Kt4

If 26 BxKt, RxB; 27 R–B7, P–Q3; 28 R–Q7, PxP; 29 PxP, R(R1)–R3; 30 R(B1)–B7, R(R3)–Kt3; Black has a satisfactory defence.

26 ...   R(R1)–R3!

The only defence! 26..., Kt–Q4; 27 R–Kt7, Kt–B2; 28 B–R3, loses a pawn.

27 R(B1)–Kt1 Kt–Q4
28 R–Kt8 ch K–R2
29 R(Kt1)–Kt7 R–B2

29..., Kt–B2; was better because after 30 R–Q8, Kt–K3; 31 R(Q8)xP, RxB!; 32 PxR, KtxP; 33 RxP, KtxR; 34 RxKt, R–K3; Black has a simple draw. After the text-move a difficult rook ending ensues.

30 RxR   KtxR
31 R–Q8   Kt–K3
32 RxP   KtxB
33 PxKt   R–K3
34 R–Q5

The ending is instructive. Black must work fast since the advance of the white king threatens to assist the passed pawn.

34 ...   P–B3
35 PxP   RxP

35..., PxP; would fail against 36 RxP, K–Kt3; 37 R–B1!, followed by R–QB1.

36 R–Q6

Even against this strong move Black has a defence. Less powerful was 36 R–Q4, R–B3; 37 R–QB4, K–Kt3; 38 K–B2, K–B3; 39 K–K3, K–K4; 40 P–KR4, P–R4!; 41 R–B2, K–Q4.

36 ...   K–Kt3
37 R–Kt6   K–B2
38 K–B2   R–K3
39 P–B6   R–K5
40 RxP   P–B5

Trying for the trap 41 K–B3, PxP! However, a simpler line was 40..., R–B5; 41 K–K3, P–R5.

41 R–R5

Tal thought for fifty minutes before sealing this move, which is the one that gives him the best chance.

41 ...   PxP ch
42 PxP   P–R5

It is doubtful whether White could have won even after 42..., R–B5; 43 RxP, RxP.

43	R–B5	PxP ch
44	KxP	R–K1
45	K–B4	R–QR1

P–Kt4 ch! was an interesting way of clinching the draw. If then 46 RxP, R–QB1; 47 R–B5, K–K3; while if 46 KxP, K–K3; and if 46 K–B5, P–Kt5! Now the game moves on into a difficult queen ending.

46	K–K5	K–K2
47	R–Q5!	

Black probably overlooked that after 47..., R–Q1; 48 RxR, KxR; 49 K–Q6!, P–Kt4; 50 P–R4, wins. After taking the RP, 48 R–Q7 ch, would drive the black king to his rear rank and the white king would reach the BP's queening square.

47	... , ,	R–R2
48	P–R4	P–Kt4
49	P–R5	P–Kt5
50	R–Kt5	P–Kt6
51	R–Kt7 ch	RxR
52	PxR	P–Kt7
53	P–Kt8=Q	P–Kt8=Q
54	Q–B7 ch	K–K7
55	Q–B8 ch	K–K2
56	Q–B7 ch	K–K1
57	K–Q6	Q–Q5 ch
58	K–B6	Q–K5 ch
59	K–Kt6	Q–Kt5 ch
60	K–R6	Q–QR5
61	K–Kt7	Q–Kt5 ch
62	Q–Kt6	Q–K2 ch
63	K–B8	Q–K5
64	Q–Kt5 ch	K–B1
65	P–R6	Q–K3 ch
66	K–B7	Q–K2 ch
67	Q–Q7	Q–B4 ch
68	Q–B6	Q–K6
69	K–Kt7	Q–K2 ch
70	K–B8	Q–K6
71	Q–B6 ch	K–Kt1
72	Q–Q8 ch	K–R2
73	Q–B7 ch	

73	...	K–R3?

The losing move. K–R1 was safe, for if 74 P–R7, Q–K5; 75 K–Kt8, Q–Kt5 ch; 76 Q–Kt7, Q–B5 ch; 77 K–R8, Q–Q5.

74	P–R7	Q–K5
75	Q–Kt6 ch!	Resigns

For if the king goes to the fourth rank, White plays 76 Q–R5 ch, and 77 P–R8=Q.

GAME 20

Tal's game against Geller was an important landmark in his uncommonly entertaining series of victories. Both players are lovers of complications and as early as the 12th move their clash was marked by combinative play, with Geller showing himself not in the least reluctant to meet Tal on his own ground. The game proceeded by a string of surprising turns until at the very climax Geller slipped and then quickly subsided.

RUY LOPEZ

	TAL	GELLER
1	P–K4	P–K4
2	Kt–KB3	Kt–QB3
3	B–Kt5	P–QR3
4	B–R4	Kt–B3
5	o–o	B–K2
6	R–K1	P–QKt4
7	B–Kt3	o–o
8	P–B3	P–Q3

9	P–KR3	Kt–QR4
10	B–B2	P–B4
11	P–Q4	B–Kt2

A new idea, instead of the usual 11 . . . ,
Q–B2; or 11 . . . , BPxP; 12 PxP, Q–B2.

12 P–QKt4!?

Not content to play the simplifying line
12 PxKP, PxP; 13 QxQ, KRxQ; 14 B–Kt5,
which assures White of a small positional
advantage. He has played the text-move
several times, rather than 12 QKt–Q2,
which causes Black no trouble, or 12 P–Q5,
which closes the centre and does not appeal
to a player who prefers open positions
with combinative possibilities.

12	. . .	PxKtP
13	PxKtP	Kt–B5
14	QKt–Q2	P–Q4

Geller complicates in his turn, for 14 . . . .
KtxKt; 15 BxKt, is somewhat to White's
advantage.

15 PxQP

An alternative was 15 KtxKt, KtPxKt; 16
PxKP, KtxP; 17 P–R3, and 18 Kt–Q4.

15 . . . PxP

Tal considers that after 15 . . . , KtxP; 16
KtxKt, PxKt; 17 KtxP, KtxP; 18 KtxQBP,
KtxB; 19 QxKt, R–B1; 20 Q–Q3, Black
has insufficient compensation for his lost
pawn.

| 16 | KtxKt | PxKt |
| 17 | QxP | BxKtP |

Black has to decide which of the pawns
to take. If 17 . . . , KtxP; 18 Q–K4, P–Kt3;
19 B–R6, R–K1; 20 B–R4, Kt–B6; 21
QxQB, KtxB; 22 Q–B6, White gets a decisive advantage, while if 17 . . . , BxQP;
18 Kt–K5, BxP; 19 R–Q1, White has a
strong initiative, so the text-move is probably best.

18 R–Kt1!

White's initiative would have evaporated
if he had withdrawn the rook, so he prefers to sacrifice the exchange, after which
his two bishops will come into their own.
Black must accept the offer, for if 18 . . . ,
KtxP; 19 BxP ch, KxB; 20 Kt–Kt5 ch,
K–Kt1; 21 Q–R4, Kt–B3; 22 RxB, Q–Q4;
23 Kt–B3, White has a pull.

| 18 | . . . | BxR |
| 19 | RxB | R–K1 |

Theoretically best, but in view of White's
attacking intentions Geller might have
done better with 19 . . . , QxP; 20 QxQ,
KtxQ; 21 KtxB, QR–Kt1; 22 RxR, RxR;
forcing an end-game which would probably end in a draw. But Geller is not out
for simplifications!

20 P–Q6

To answer R–K7 with 21 QxP.

20 . . . Q–B1

21 B-Kt5!

21 R-B7, Q-K3; 22 B-Kt5, Kt-Q4; 23 R-B5, Kt-B6; allowed Black good counter-play.

21 ...   R-K7!

A worthy riposte! He would have done himself no good by accepting the sacrifice: 21..., QxR; 22 BxKt, PxB; 23 Q-R4, and now either 23..., BxP ch; 24 KxB, Q-Kt3 ch; 25 Kt-Q4!, QxP; 26 QxP ch, K-B1; 27 Q-R6 ch, winning the queen or mating, or 23..., P-B4; Q-Kt5 ch, K-B1; 25 Q-B6, K-Kt1; 26 BxP, with a decisive attack. Now BxP ch is threatened.

22 R-B7

Necessary, since 22 KtxB, RxKt ch; 23 K-R2, QxR; 24 BxKt, PxB; 25 Q-R4, P-B4; 26 BxP, P-B3; does not yield White any break-through.

22 ...   Q-K3
23 KtxB

The exchange is now feasible.

23 ...   RxKt ch
24 K-R2   R-Q1

He has to watch the strong QP and the threatened R-K7. Insufficient is 24..., Kt-Q2; 25 B-QR4!

25 BxKt

Now 25 R-K7, fails after 27..., QxR; 28 BxP ch, K-R1! White could recover the exchange by 25 BxP ch, KxB; 26 R-K7, QxP; 27 QxQ, RxQ; 28 RxR, but Black then has the better game after 28..., Kt-Q2.

25 ...   PxB?

A grave mistake, throwing away this delightful game which has been so well contested on both sides so far. Correct was 25..., QxB; 26 QxQ, PxQ; 27 P-Q7, producing an interesting position which requires care, for if 27..., K-B1; 28 BxP, R-K7; 29 K-Kt3, RxRP; 30 B-B5, White's passed pawns are stronger than Black's, especially the KRP. Black however can obtain the draw by 27..., K-Kt2!; 28 B-B5, R-K4; 29 R-B8, RxB; 30 RxR, R-Q4.

26 R-K7   QxP

He has no good move, QxR losing against 27 Q-Kt4 ch.

27	QxQ	RxQ
28	RxR	R-Q7
29	R-QB1	RxP
30	B-K4	RxP
31	RxP	P-QR4
32	R-B8 ch	K-Kt2
33	R-B7	Resigns

GAME 21

Tal gained a big positional advantage by energetic play against Furman, who tried to resuscitate an old-fashioned defence. Furman sacrificed a pawn under pressure without adequate compensation, except that Tal, carried away by dreams of a possible combination, made a serious error and ended up with the worse game. He was lucky, however, since Furman then overstepped the time limit. If fortune is said to favour the brave, there is no doubt it also favours the strong.

RUY LOPEZ

	TAL	FURMAN
1	P–K4	P–K4
2	Kt–KB3	Kt–QB3
3	B–Kt5	Kt–B3
4	P–Q4	PxP
5	P–K5	Kt–K5
6	Q–K2	

In theory White's strongest move in this variation is to castle on the 4th move. In the variation chosen here Pachman's book only considers 6 o–o, and gives it as leading to an equal game. Pachman's analysis, however, does not consider the manoeuvre Q–K2 and R–Q1.

6	...	Kt–B4
7	o–o	B–K2
8	R–Q1	o–o
9	BxKt	KtPxB
10	KtxP	Q–K1
11	Kt–QB3	P–B3
12	Kt–B5	B–Q1

Worth considering was 12..., PxP; 13 QxP, Kt–K3.

| 13 | Q–B4 ch | Kt–K3 |

| 14 | Kt–Q4! | PxP |
| 15 | KtxKt | P–Q4!? |

Preferring the sacrifice of a pawn to recapturing on K3 with a ruined pawn structure.

16	KtxBP!	Q–B2
17	Kt(B3)xP	PxKt
18	KtxP	QxP ch
19	K–R1	B–K3
20	B–K3	Q–B2
21	Q–K4	R–B1
22	P–B3	R–K1
23	R–Q2	R–Kt1

Black's pawn sacrifice gave him counter-play for a short time but now it can be seen that he has insufficient compensation. The simplest way for White now to increase his advantage was 24 P–B4, but Tal is tempted to introduce a combinative motif.

24	QR–Q1	B–B4
25	Q–QR4	B–QKt3
26	R–KB1	

This game is a good example of the faults in Tal's play. He goes in for complications when once again he could have asserted his advantage by simple means. The obvious move was 26 P–B4, and then if 26..., R(K1)–KB1; 27 BxB, PxB; 28 Q–QKt4!

26	...	Q–R4
27	BxB	PxB
28	R(Q2)–KB2	B–Q6!

Clearly the rooks were better placed on the Q file than they are on the KB file. Now Black can start counter-play after 29 R–K1, by R–KB1.

29 P-KKt4?

Fascinated by what would be a very nice combination if only it were capable of realization: 29..., Q-R6; 30 QxR ch!, RxQ; 31 R-B8 ch!, RxR; 32 Kt-K7 ch, K-R1; 33 RxR mate, while 29..., Q-Kt3; would allow the overpowering Q-Q7. But it is all a mirage, ruined by Black's simple answer which wins the exchange.

29	...	Q-R5!
30	KtxP	BxR
31	RxB	R-KB1

Now White is able to develop threats owing to the undefended back rank. 31..., Q-K2; was far better.

32	Q-B4 ch	K-R1
33	Kt-Q7	RxR ch
34	QxR	R-K1
35	KtxP!	Q-K2
36	Kt-B3	Q-K5
37	K-Kt2	QxP ch
38	K-B2	

Black here overstepped his time and lost, though with White's material balance he could hardly have had more than a draw at best.

GAME 22

Tal's style is no insurance against peril. With his perpetual search for tension he is constantly taking risks, and even more so than usual in an exceptionally strong field like that assembled for the XXVth Championship. For this reason he lost three games in the tournament – to Korchnoi, Boleslavsky and Bannik – and reached a situation where he had to win his last two games to be sure of finishing first.

In one, against Gipslis, he managed it without great difficulty, for his young opponent, regarded in his home town of Riga as Tal's most dangerous rival, chose an opening of doubtful value, which was just what Tal required. A barely discernable error on the 9th move led to Gipslis' defeat, Tal exploiting the position with fluent elegance and the superior placing of his forces being achieved with all his customary energy.

SICILIAN DEFENCE

	TAL	GIPSLIS
1	P-K4	P-QB4
2	Kt-KB3	P-K3
3	P-Q4	PxP
4	KtxP	P-QR3
5	Kt-QB3	

The attempt to refute Black's play by 5 P-QB4, raises problems for both sides which have never been fully solved.

5	...	P-QKt4

5..., Q-B2; is certainly more prudent.

6	B-Q3	B-Kt2
7	0-0	Q-B2
8	R-K1	

At Riga in 1958 Krogius played 8 Q-K2, against Korchnoi, so that after P-Kt5 he could withdraw the knight to Q1. The game continued 8..., Kt-QB3; 9 KtxKt, PxKt; 10 P-QR4, P-Kt5; 11 Kt-Q1, P-QB4; 12 Kt-K3, and White had the advantage. But later at the same tournament the Boleslavsky-Kotov game revealed an improvement for Black with 8..., Kt-KB3; 9 B-Q2, Kt-B3; 10 KtxKt, QxKt; 11 P-QR3, B-B4; and the position is level. Tal's move is more effective, as will appear after White's 13th move.

8	...	Kt-QB3

8..., Kt-KB3; was worth considering. In the game Durasevic-Taimanov at Zagreb, 1958, a draw was agreed after 8..., Kt-KB3; 9 P-K5, Kt-Q4; 10 B-Q2, KtxKt; 11 BxKt, Kt-B3; 12 KtxKt, BxKt; though

White would have had chances after 13 Q–Kt4, because of his more open position.

| 9 | KtxKt | QxKt? |

It could hardly have been foreseen that this move would create great difficulties for Black, but since that is so, 9 ..., PxKt; was essential.

| 10 | P–QR4! |

Surprisingly simple and simply surprising. By the attack on the QKtP he provokes Black's reply.

| 10 | ... | P–Kt5 |

10 ..., PxP; 11 RxP, Kt–B3; 12 R–B4, Q–Kt3; 13 B–K3, was worse still.

| 11 | Kt–Q5 |

This is nothing if not surprising! With one sudden move Black can find no defence, being overshadowed by the threat of 12 B–Q2, P–QR4; 13 B–KB4, R–B1; 14 B–QKt5, Q–B4; 15 BxP ch.

| 11 | ... | Kt–B3 |

The only other possibility was o–o–o, but then after 12 Kt–K3, Black's king looks extremely exposed to attack.

| 12 | B–Q2! |

Tal now makes the most of his advantage with a few well-chosen moves.

| 12 | ... | KtxKt |

There is nothing else, for 12 ..., P–QR4; loses to 13 B–QKt5, Q–B4; 14 B–K3, Q–Q3; 15 B–KB4, P–K4; 16 BxKP.

| 13 | PxKt |

The difference between 8 Q–K2, and 8 R–K1, is now apparent. Black cannot now play QxP; because as Tal has played it, there is the reply 14 B–K4.

| 13 | ... | Q–B4 |

14 B–K4!

Simple but still very fine. The threat is 15 PxP, winning a pawn, and if 14 .... BxP; then 15 B–K3, Q–B3; 16 BxB, QxB; 17 QxQ, PxQ; 18 B–Kt5 dis. ch. Black therefore creates an escape square for his K.

| 14 | ... | P–B4 |
| 15 | B–KB3 |

Much better than 15 BxBP, BxP; 16 Q–R5 ch, K–Q1; with no evident advantage to White.

| 15 | ... | BxP |

Relatively best. Against 15 ..., o–o–o; White has the decisive 16 B–Kt5, and then if 16 ..., R–K1; 17 PxP, PxP; 18 BxB ch, KxB; 19 Q–Q7 ch, winning the rook, or if 16 ..., B–K2; 17 BxB, QxB; 18 P–Q6.

Q-B3; 19 BxB ch, KxB; 20 Q-B3 ch, with an irresistible attack.

16   BxP

Recovering his pawn and thus further emphasising his superiority.

16 ...   BxB

The following were alternative possibilities: 16 . . . , QxB; 17 QxB, and now either 17 . . . , R-Q1; 18 QxBP, QxKtP; 19 QR-Kt1, QxR?; 20 B-R5 ch, P-Kt3; 21 BxP ch, or 17 . . . , R-QKt1; 18 QR-Q1, Q-K2; 19 B-R5 ch, P-Kt3 (K-Q1; 20 Q-R5 ch). 20 Q-K5, and wins.

17 QxB   Q-B1
18 B-B3   K-B2
19 QR-Q1

Preparing the final stroke by threatening RxP ch.

19 ...   B-K2

If Black could only find time to castle in effect by R-B1 and K-Kt1, he might still hold the game.

20 P-KKt4!

Obtaining a dominating position on the vital files.

20 ...   R-B1

What else? 20 . . . , Q-B3; 21 QxQ, PxQ; 22 PxP, PxP; 23 R-Q7, KR-K1; 24 B-Kt4, or

20 . . . , Q-B4; 21 R-K5, winning in each case.

21 PxP   K-Kt1
22 Q-Kt2   B-B3

If 22 . . . , R-B2; 23 RxQP, QxR; 24 PxP, QxP; 25 QxR ch, R-B1; 26 QxR ch.

23 BxB   RxB
24 RxQP

The simultaneous attack on QR1 and KKt2, finely elaborated and carried through with great energy, decides the game.

24 ...   QxR
25 QxR ch   R-B1
26 QxP   Resigns

GAME 23

Before the last round Petrosian and Tal led with $11\frac{1}{2}$ points and, as so often in Russian championships, there was intense competition among a whole cluster at the front. Bronstein was $\frac{1}{2}$ point and Averbach and Spassky 1 point behind. Naturally the Spassky–Tal game became the centre of interest. Tal was somewhat lucky to beat his great rival; the Leningrad champion tried for complications and so far from accepting a pawn sacrifice he offered one; Tal's position looked hazardous, but a stout defence brought equality and when Spassky tried for too much. Tal reaped the fruits of victory. Since Petrosian could only draw, the destination of the Championship was decided.

NIMZO-INDIAN DEFENCE

SPASSKY	TAL
1 P-Q4	Kt-KB3
2 P-QB4	P-K3
3 Kt-QB3	B-Kt5
4 P-QR3	BxKt ch
5 PxB	P-B4

6	P-K3	Kt-B3
7	B-Q3	P-K4

White's choice of the critical Samisch variation indicated an intention of playing to win. Black equally plays an active game as shown by this double-edged advance of the KP.

8	Kt-K2	P-K5
9	B-Kt1	P-QKt3

Preferring a counter-attack on White's QBP to passive defence of his own KP by o-o and R-K1.

10	Kt-Kt3	B-R3

11	P-B3

Usually regarded as the most effective way of meeting Black's line of defence. There are fewer difficulties for Black after 11 KtxP, KtxKt; 12 BxKt, BxP; because of the favourable end-game following 13 PxP, PxP; 14 BxKt, PxB; 15 QxQ ch. Then again White could play to win a pawn by 11 Q-R4, Kt-QR4; 12 PxP, BxP; 13 KtxP, KtxKt; 14 BxKt, R-QB1; 15 PxP, PxP; but Black gets sufficient counter-play. No more effective is 11 Q-R4, Kt-QR4; 12 KtxP, because after 12..., KtxKt (not BxP; 13 Kt-Q6 ch); 13 BxKt, R-QB1; Black regains the pawn with a good game.

11	...	BxP

Not 11..., KPxP; 12 QxP, BxP; when White gets a dangerous attack by Kt-B5 and P-K4.

12	Kt-B5

An artificial manoeuvre. After the simple PxKP Black would have difficulty in finding counter-chances in view of White's strong centre and his pair of bishops.

12	...	o-o
13	Kt-Q6	B-Q6
14	BxB	PxB
15	QxP	PxP
16	BPxP	Kt-K1
17	Kt-B5	P-Q4
18	P-QR4	

18	...	Kt-Q3!

This excellent move renders the threatened 19 B-R3, ineffective because that move would now be answered by 19..., KtxKt; 20 BxR, Q-Kt4! Thus Black secures a satisfactory position.

19	KtxKt	QxKt
20	B-R3	Kt-Kt5
21	Q-Kt3	P-QR4
22	o-o	

QR-Kt1 is not effective because of 22..., KR-B1; 23 o-o, R-B5.

22	...	KR–B1	
23	QR–B1	Q–K3	
24	BxKt	PxB	
25	K–B2	Q–Q3	
26	P–R3	K–B1	

An inaccurate move which allows White to obtain control of the QB-file. Correct was 26 . . ., R–B3; but Tal's explosive personality is hardly likely to be patient enough to find such a move.

27	R–B2!	RxR	
28	QxR	P–Kt3	
29	R–B1	Q–Q2	
30	Q–B6	QxQ	
31	RxQ	R–R3	
32	P–R5!		

Now 32 . . ., RxP; 33 RxQKtP, would yield a favourable end-game for White. Tal avoids this by a small combination which leads to an ending with fresh queens.

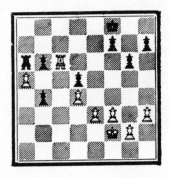

32	...	P–Kt6!	
33	PxP	P–Kt7	
34	P–Kt7!	P–Kt8=Q	
35	R–B8 ch	K–Kt2	
36	P–Kt8=Q	R–R7 ch	
37	K–Kt3	Q–K8 ch	
38	K–R2	QxP	
39	R–Kt8 ch	K–B3	
40	Q–Q6 ch	Q–K3	
41	Q–B4 ch	Q–B4	
42	Q–Q6 ch	Q–K3	
43	Q–Kt3	Q–K6	

44	P–R4	R–K7	
45	Q–Q6 ch	Q–K3	

Here the game was adjourned. The position of the black K induced Spassky to try for a win which the course of the game shows not to be there. The trouble is that Spassky refuses to admit the fruitlessness of his efforts.

46	Q–B4 ch	Q–B4	
47	Q–R6	K–K2	
48	Q–B8 ch	K–B3	
49	Q–Kt7 ch	K–K2	
50	R–QR8	Q–Q2	
51	Q–B8 ch	K–B3	
52	R–R6 ch	R–K3	
53	Q–R8 ch	K–K2	
54	R–R8	R–K8	
55	K–Kt3	P–R4	
56	K–B2	R–K3	
57	R–QB8	R–Q3	
58	Q–B8 ch	K–B3	
59	R–K8	R–K3	
60	Q–R8 ch	K–B4	
61	Q–R6	K–B3	

Naturally not 61 . . ., RxR?; because of 62 Q–Kt5 ch, K–K3; 63 Q–K5 mate.

62	Q–R8 ch	K–B4	
63	R–Q8		

By not taking the draw even now White prepares to lose.

63	...	Q–B3
64	R–QB8ꝑ	Q–R3
65	K–Kt3	Q–Q3 ch
66	K–R3	R–K8

The boot is now on the other foot! It is White's king which is in danger, and the danger is mortal because his associates cannot get back to help in his defence.

67	P–Kt3	R–KKt8
68	P–B4	R–K8
69	R–B2	Q–K3!
70	R–B2	R–R8 ch
71	K–Kt2	Q–K5 ch
72	R–B3	

| 72 | ... | K–Kt5 |

The once harassed king supplies the finishing stroke to his rival!

| 73 | Q–B8 ch | P–B4 |
| | Resigns | |

INTER-ZONAL TOURNAMENT FOR THE
WORLD CHAMPIONSHIP

At Portoroz in the autumn of 1958 the Yugoslav Chess Federation organized the Inter-zonal Tournament, a gathering of most of the finest players of the world. Tal was now regarded as one of the favourites in spite of the alarming quality of the opposition and his devotees were not disappointed, for yet once again the first prize found its way to Mikhail Tal!

For him Portoroz was such a triumph that the ranks of those who still doubted became thin indeed. A first prize in such a tournament is beyond being explained away as an accident for, apart from Botvinnik, Keres and Smyslov, they were all there, the whole of the championship field. Tal played brilliantly and with his usual fire and energy, which is as much as to say he well deserved his victory.

GAME 24

Tal's game against Filip was delightful in spite of its inaccuracies and omissions. The king's side attack with its intention of achieving a central break-through is much to be admired. After Black's faulty 32nd move, which lost a piece without compensation, it was all over.

RUY LOPEZ

	TAL	FILIP
1	P–K4	P–K4
2	Kt–KB3	Kt–QB3
3	B–Kt5	P–QR3
4	B–R4	Kt–B3
5	O–O	B–K2
6	R–K1	P–QKt4
7	B–Kt3	P–Q3
8	P–B3	Kt–QR4
9	P–KR3	P–B4
10	B–B2	Q–B2
11	P–Q4	O–O
12	QKt–Q2	

A well-known position in the close variation of the Lopez, from which many choices are open to both sides. Filip chooses one of the oldest.

12	...	Kt–B3
13	PxBP	PxP
14	Kt–B1	B–Q3

Since White aims in this variation to occupy Black's Q4 and KB4 by Kt–K3–Q5 and Kt–R4–B5, Black must defend these points. The text-move deriving from Botvinnik, plans to do this by following up with Kt–K2.

15 Kt–R4

Smyslov introduced this move in the 14th game of his 1957 match with Botvinnik and the knight gained in effectiveness after Botvinnik's 15 ..., P–Kt3. The play at Portoroz showed that Black's next was an improvement on Botvinnik's move. The old move here for White used to be 15 B–Kt5, but it has been found to be satis-

factorily answered by 15..., Kt–K1; 16
Kt–K3, P–B3; 17 Kt–Q5, Q–Kt2 or Q–B2.

| 15 ... | Kt–K2 |
| 16 Q–B3 | |

If 16 B–Kt5, Black's best defence is 16...,
Kt–K1; 17 Kt–B5, B–K3!; and 18 ...,
P–B3. Black need have no fear of exchanging the bishop on Q3 because it is only
serving in a defensive role.

| 16 ... | R–Q1 |

In a previous meeting between the two at
Reykjavik in 1957 Filip here played 16...,
B–K3; and the game was equal after 17
Kt–Kt3, Q–B3; 18 Kt(R4)–B5, KtxKt,
19 KtxKt, BxKt; 20 QxB, Kt–K1. Possibly
Filip deviated from the previous line
through fear of running into a prepared
innovation.

| 17 Kt–K3 | Q–Kt2 |

Black has slightly the poorer game owing
to the awkwardness of the whole variation.
The text was played to avoid the lines
of the Averbach–Neikirch game in the
same tournament when White got an advantage after 17..., Q–B3; 18 P–B4!,
Kt–K1; 19 B–Kt3, P–Kt5; 20 Kt–Q5,
Q–Kt2; 21 B–R4, Kt–B2; 22 B–KKt5,
Kt(B2)xKt; 23 BPxKt. But now after the
exchanges on Black's KB4 White will be
able to attack along the KKt file and
Black's defence will be difficult.

18 P–KKt4	P–B5
19 Kt(K3)–B5	KtxKt
20 KtxKt	BxKt
21 KtPxB!	K–R1
22 K–R2?	

A slight inaccuracy which tarnishes a so far
well-played game. K–R1 would have led
to a forced win, whereas the value of the
break-through is somewhat doubtful after
the text-move.

| 22 ... | P–R3? |

Also inaccurate! The pawn move is not
necessary and only weakens the king's
position. 22..., Kt–K1 and 23....
P–B3; gave more chances of a successful
defence.

23 R–KKt1	Q–K2
24 B–Q2	B–B4
25 QR–Q1	R–Q2
26 Q–Kt3	Q–B1
27 K–R1	

If the king had only been on KR1 in the
first place, a sacrifice on Black's KR3
would now have been strong.

| 27 ... | QR–Q1 |

28 BxP!

This sacrifice is not effective against the
correct defence, but should one query it
when it gives White the chance of winning
in the ensuing complications? In other continuations the transition to an end-game
would favour Black.

| 28 ... | PxB |
| 29 QxP | B–K2? |

Black could have put his finger on the
weak spot in the sacrifice by playing
29..., Q–K2!; his game would be favourable after 30 Q–B4, Kt–R2 (an analysis in the *Deutsche Schachzeitung* suggests
that K–R2! is still better); 31 QxP, Q–B3;
or 31 RxR, RxR; 32 P–K5, P–B3; 33 P–K6,

R–Q1! Tal now obtains a powerful centre and is able to deliver an overwhelming attack.

30	R–Q4!	RxR
31	PxR	K–R2
32	R–Q1	Kt–K1?

Another good example of Tal's "luck." Black is in difficulties with his defence against the repeated threats of a central pawn advance and the opening of the bishop's diagonal. Exhausted by his consideration of the various possibilities, Filip failed to find the defence 32 . . . , Kt–Q2; and 33 . . . , P–B3; after which he still had a chance of holding out. That is not to say that he would not still have been in trouble and in many lines might well have had to reckon on giving back the piece.

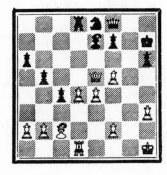

33 P–B6!

White's bishop comes into action at last. Black's position is untenable.

33 . . . KtxP

BxP was no better.

34	Q–B5 ch	K–R1
35	P–K5	Q–Kt2
36	PxKt	BxP
37	R–KKt1	B–Kt4
38	P–B4	Resigns

GAME 25

The Soviet school of chess has a long tradition of development and now exerts a wide influence everywhere. It seems to produce masters almost as if out of a mould, one of the best being Mikhail Tal. In him the basic concept of the Soviet school is most fully manifested, namely the dynamic approach which seeks a fight even at the cost of a weakness or a sacrifice of material. Other characteristics of the Soviet school, the creation and shrewd exploitation of positional advantages, are equally manifest in Tal's play. The motif of the following game is the utilization of White' weaknesses on the queen's side.

SICILIAN DEFENCE

	SZABÓ	TAL
1	P–K4	P–QB4
2	Kt–KB3	P–Q3
3	B–Kt5 ch	B–Q2
4	BxB ch	QxB
5	O–O	Kt–QB3
6	P–B3	Kt–B3
7	R–K1	P–K3

In the B–QKt5 variation of the Sicilian, Black frequently fianchettoes his KB, but after 6 P–B3, Tal considers it may do better on the other diagonal.

8	P–Q4	PxP
9	PxP	P–Q4
10	P–K5	

With a position reminiscent of the French Defence, except that Black has gained by having to face no active white bishop on Q3 and is not burdened with a caged QB of his own.

| 10 | . . . | Kt–K5 |
| 11 | Kt–QB3 | |

Szabó is as activated by the dynamic approach as any of the Soviet masters, many of whom he has in consequence been able to beat. Here he accepts the weakness of his QBP for the sake of an initiative on the king's side and on the QKt file, though in retrospect it can be seen that 11 QKt–Q2, would have been better because after 11 . . . ; KtxKt; 12 BxKt, B–K2; the position would have been essentially the same without the pawn weakness. Admittedly he would not have had an open QKt file but, as will appear, this is insufficient to compensate for a bad pawn skeleton.

11	. . .	KtxKt
12	PxKt	

Tal's exploitation of this weakness and his neat thwarting of White's attempts to increase his activity make the game a most instructive one.

12	. . .	B–K2
13	Kt–Kt5	P–KR3
14	Q–R5	

Kt–R3 was worth considering so that if Black castled on the K-side a pawn attack could be launched with P–KB4 and P–Kt4.

14	. . .	BxKt
15	BxB	Kt–K2
16	B–Q2	O–O
17	P–QR4	

According to Tal, there were good chances now by sacrificing the bishop, and he gives the following variations: 17 BxP, PxB; 18 QxRP, Q–Q1! (18 . . ., Kt–B4; 19 Q–Kt5 ch, Kt–Kt2; – if K–R2; 20 R–K3, KtxR; 21 Q–R5 ch, it is a draw – 20 R–K3, Q–Q1; 21 Q–R6, is merely a transposition); 19 R–K3, Kt–B4; 20 Q–R5, KtxR; 21 PxKt, Q–K2; 22 Q–Kt4 ch, K–R2; 23 Q–R5 ch, K–Kt2; 24 Q–Kt4 ch, K–R3; 25 R–KB1, P–B4! (R–KKt1?; 26 R–B6 ch, R–Kt3; 27 Q–R4 ch, K–Kt2; 28 RxR ch, winning); 26 PxP e. p., RxP; 27 Q–R4 ch, drawing by perpetual check. Or instead of the above, 20 . . ., Kt–Kt2; 21 Q–R6, P–B4; 22 R–Kt3, Q–K2; 23 P–KB4, with

complicated play. Whatever Tal may say, one could reasonably suspect that, like Szabó, he would avoid these lines because of the many forced drawing lines involved. Szabó accordingly prepares a Q-side offensive, but the idea is defeated by Tal's exemplary play and the advance of the QRP will soon be found to have weakened the pawn structure still further, so that White finds himself on that road to hell which is paved with good intentions.

17	. . .	P–B4
18	P–KB4?	

A grave mistake which leaves his bishop quite useless. The more active knight tips the scales on the Q-side. The only chance of counter-play lay in 18 PxP e. p., RxP; 19 R–K2.

18	. . .	QR–B1
19	KR–Kt1	R–B5
20	Q–Q1	KR–B1
21	P–R5	Kt–B3
22	Q–Kt3	R–B2
23	R–Kt2	K–R2!

A necessary preparation for his plan. If 23 . . ., P–R3; at once, then 24 Q–Kt6, Kt–K2; 25 Q–Q6, R(B5)–B3 (Q–K1 now fails against QxP ch); 26 QxQ, RxQ; 27 QR–Kt1, and he has equalized.

24	P–R3	P–R3!

25	Q–Kt6!

A most instructive situation. Black intends to place his Kt on QKt4 so as to add decisive weight to his attack on the QBP and the text-move is part of White's counter to this plan. For the next ten moves both players fence around this possibility.

| 25 | . . . | Kt–K2! |

Threatening Kt–B1–R2–Kt4 once again.

| 26 | Q–Q6 | Q–K1! |

Introducing a combinative element into the play. White cannot take the KP on account of the loss of his queen, but he threatens to have it next move.

27	R–Kt6	R(B5)–B3
28	RxR	QxR
29	R–Kt1	R–Q2
30	Q–Kt4	

The ending would have been hopeless after 30 QxQ, KtxQ; 31 R–R1, Kt–R2; with Black continuing with Kt–Kt4, R–B2 and R–B5.

| 30 | . . . | Kt–B1 |
| 31 | P–Kt4 | |

The black knight will reach QKt4 at last, so White starts an attack on the king as his last chance, but Tal successfully nips this attack in the bud too.

31	. . .	P–KKt3
32	Q–B8	R–Kt2
33	K–B2	

He could have prevented the following incursion of the black queen by Q–Kt4 but then weakness on the Q-side would have cost him the game.

33	. . .	Q–B5!
34	R–Kt2	Kt–R2
35	R–Kt6	

Still delaying Black's Kt–Kt4 by hitting the KP, but now the white king is stripped of defenders and first the queen and then the knight gets at him.

35	. . .	Kt–B3
36	K–K1	Q–Q6!
37	P–Kt5	PxP
38	PxP	

| 38 | . . . | KtxRP! |

He can now even let the KP go.

39	RxKP	Kt–B5
40	B–B1	QxP ch
41	K–Q1	QxP ch
42	K–K2	Q–K5 ch
43	K–Q1	Q–B6 ch
44	K–B2	

After 44 K–K1, Q–R8 ch; 45 K–B2, QxB; he cannot play 46 R–K7, on account of 46 . . . , Q–K6 ch; forcing the white K to the KKt file, when Black wins the rook by QxKtP.

44	. . .	Q–K7 ch
45	K–B3	P–Q5 ch!
46	K–Kt4	P–R4 ch
47	K–B5	R–B2 ch
48	K–Kt5	KtxP dis. ch
49	K–Kt6	R–B3 ch
	Resigns	

GAME 26

In the game against Panno the complications are fantastic even by Tal's own standard. The game is in many ways reminiscent of the Tal–Geller game in the XXVth Championship where it was also a pawn move that introduced the complications. This game is one of splendid attacks, unwavering defence and in the end an error without which it would have ended with honours even. In his analysis of the game L. Abramov describes Tal's play as follows: "Just look at Tal! How bold he is, how quick to come to a decision, how accurate in finding his way through the calculation of far-reaching lines of play. I can reveal here that the variations I quote were scribbled down by Tal without sight of the board in a matter of minutes. He wanted to go on further but as he was in a hurry to start play in another round of the tournament, I refused to delay him any longer." In presenting this game, we have made use of the analysis quoted by Abramov.

RUY LOPEZ

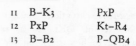

	TAL	PANNO
1	P-K4	P-K4
2	Kt-KB3	Kt-QB3
3	B-Kt5	P-QR3
4	B-R4	Kt-B3
5	O-O	B-K2
6	R-K1	P-QKt4
7	B-Kt3	P-Q3
8	P-B3	O-O
9	P-KR3	Kt-Q2

Recent research has made this line of defence playable. The intention is to regroup by Kt-Kt3 and B-B3.

| 10 | P-Q4 | Kt-Kt3 |

Preferable to B-B3, which is answered by the strong move 11 P-QR4!

11	B-K3	PxP
12	PxP	Kt-R4
13	B-B2	P-QB4

| 14 | P-K5 |

Starting the complications. Tal regards this move as the only one which helps White to mobilize his pieces, though in fact the quieter 14 P-QKt3, comes into consideration as well.

| 14 | ... | PxKP! |

Good play. 14 ..., PxQP; 15 BxP, favours White, while 14 ..., Kt(R4)-B5; is met with 15 PxQP, QxP; 16 B-Kt5, BxB; 17 KtxB, P-R3; 18 Q-R5, QxP; 19 QxP ch!

| 15 | KtxP | P-B4 |
| 16 | Q-Q3 | Kt(Kt3)-B5 |

Safer was P-Kt3 followed by 17 B-R6, KtxKt (or R-K1; 18 KtxBP!?, QxP);

18 PxKt, QxQ; 19 BxQ, R–Q1. with adequate counter-play.

| 17 | B–Kt3! | P–B5 |
| 18 | B–Q2 | KtxKB |

If 18..., B–B4; 19 BxKt, QxB; 20 Q–QB3, QxQ; 21 KtxQ.

(See diagram on page 70.)

19	Kt–B6!	KtxR!
20	KtxQ	B–B4!
21	Q–KB3	QRxKt
22	RxB	BxKt
23	BxP	

A most extraordinary position! Black has a material advantage but White's pieces are better co-ordinated. Black cannot now play 23..., PxP; because of 24 P–QKt3, P–Q6; 25 Q–Kt4. Nevertheless, he has to bring his pieces back to safety and his decision is therefore the right one.

23	...	RxP!
24	Q–Kt4	B–Kt3
25	Q–K6 ch	B–B2
26	Q–B5	Kt–B7!

The obvious-looking B–Kt3 would have been a bad mistake because of the delightful continuation 27 RxP ch, KxR; 28 B–R6 ch!, KxB; 29 QxR ch, K–R4; 30 QxP ch, winning the second rook and with it the game.

| 27 | P–QKt3 | B–Kt3 |

27..., R–Q8 ch; 28 K–R2, Kt–Q7; as suggested by some commentators, would

only have helped White because after 29 BxKt, RxB; 30 QxP, Black will have great difficulty in salvaging his knight.

28 RxP ch!

No longer as decisive as in the note to the 27th move because the rook on Q5 is defended. It is still the most effective continuation, however, since only the most accurate defence can keep Black alive.

28	...	KxR
29	B–R6 ch	KxB
30	QxR ch	K–Kt4
31	PxKt	PxP
32	P–Kt3!	

Even after the simplification he is still combining! The text prepares a mating net.

| 32 | ... | B–K5! |

Black is also playing for a mate!

| 33 | P–R4 ch | K–Kt5! |

If 33..., K–Kt3; 34 P–B3, B–Q4; 35 P–Kt4!

| 34 | K–R2 | B–B4! |

Even in time trouble Panno finds the correct line. Should White now try 35 P–B3 ch, KxP; 36 QxB ch, he will be hard put to it to hold Black's passed pawn after 36..., K–K6; 37 QxRP, P–B6!

35	Q–B6	P–R3
36	Q–K5	R–K5
37	Q–Kt7 ch	K–B6

If K–R4; 38 Q–B7 ch, B–Kt3 (K–Kt5; 3)
P–B3 ch); 39 Q–B3 ch, R–Kt5; 40 K–R3.
and wins.

38	Q–B3 ch	Kt–K6
39	K–Kt1	B–Kt5
40	PxKt	P–KR4
41	Q–K1!	

| 41 | ... | RxP? |

Panno's only mistake, which is sufficient to
cost him the game. By R–K3 he could have
obtained a position so solid as to ensure the
draw.

| 42 | Q–B1 ch | K–K5 |

Not 42 ..., KxP?; 43 Q–B2 ch, K–R6; 44
Q–R2 mate.

43	QxP ch	K–B6
44	Q–B1 ch	K–K5
45	QxRP	K–Q5

Black could have caused White more trouble
by 45 ..., RxP ch; 46 K–B2, R–B6 ch;
47 K–Kt2, K–Q4; since he would then
have been able to hold up the advance of
the QRP. Even so he is drifting into a
position of near-Zugzwang and in the end
White must triumph.

| 46 | Q–Q6 ch | K–B5 |
| 47 | P–R4 | R–K8 ch |

48	K–B2	R–K7 ch
49	K–B1	R–QR7
50	Q–R6 ch	K–Q5
51	P–R5	P–B5
52	Q–Kt6 ch	K–Q4

Not K–Q6; 53 Q–Kt1 ch. It is already clear
that White's passed pawn is stronger than
Black's.

53	P–R6	R–R8 ch
54	K–B2	P–B6
55	P–R7	P–B7
56	Q–Kt3 ch	K–Q3
57	Q–Q3 ch	Resigns

For after K–K3; 58 Q–K4 ch, he cannot
face either 58 ..., K–B3 (or Q3); 59
Q–Q4 ch, or 58 ..., K–B2; 59 QxP, RxP;
60 Q–R7 ch.

GAME 27

The game against Rossetto is again peculiarly characteristic of Tal. A pawn
sacrifice and then a piece sacrifice follow
each other without apparent result. Tal recovers the piece but remains a pawn down.
Then with another pawn sacrifice he gains
time to regroup his pieces, forces a weakness in Rossetto's king's position and then
develops a decisive attack which swamps
his opponent's king like a tidal wave.

KING'S INDIAN DEFENCE

ROSSETTO   TAL

1	P–QB4	Kt–KB3
2	Kt–KB3	P–KKt3
3	P–KKt3	B–Kt2
4	B–Kt2	o–o
5	o–o	P–Q3
6	P–Q4	Kt–B3
7	Kt–B3	P–QR3
8	P–Q5	Kt–QR4
9	Q–Q3	

In this variation of the King's Indian, Black
aims to obtain play on the queen's side by
P–B4 and, after due preparation, P–QKt4.

White's usual line is 9 Kt–Q2, but equally he can play 9 P–Kt3, because of the continuation 9 . . . , KtxQP; 10 KtxKt, BxR; 11 B–Q2! The queen move selected here in no way solves White's problems.

9	. . .	P–B4
10	P–K4	P–K3!
11	P–KR3	PxP
12	BPxP	

Black's central counter-play has exposed the weakness of 9 Q–Q3. If 12 KPxP, in order to prevent P–QKt4, Black has the move 12 . . . , B–B4.

12	. . .	P–QKt4
13	B–B4	P–Kt5
14	Kt–Q1	R–K1
15	R–K1	

Kt–Q2, in order to control QB4, was worth considering.

15	. . .	P–B5
16	Q–B2	R–R2
17	B–K3	QR–K2
18	Kt–Q2	

| 18 | . . . | P–Kt6!? |

A startling pawn sacrifice, which appears to favour White owing to the weakness of Black's QRP after the opening of the QR file and the fact that his QBP can also be attacked by R–R4.

| 19 | PxP | KtxKtP |
| 20 | R–R4 | |

| 20 | . . . | KtxQP! |

Deeply and accurately calculated. He is bound to recover the piece.

21	PxKt	B–B4
22	QxP	KtxKt
23	QxP	Kt–K5

Black, for the time being at least, remains a pawn down without adequate compensation, but the position is full of the tactical opportunities which suit Tal so well.

| 24 | Q–Kt6 | Q–B1 |
| 25 | P–KKt4? | |

Creating a weakness which will bring its due retribution. Better was 25 K–R2, though then Tal would have built up the pressure with P–R4 and B–K4.

25	. . .	Kt–B4
26	R–R7	RxR
27	QxR	Kt–Q6
28	R–B1	B–K5

After three moves he takes the bishop out of jeopardy.

| 29 | Q–R3 | BxB |

Weakening the white squares round the white king.

| 30 | KxB | Q–B5! |
| 31 | QxP | |

After the obvious 31 Kt–B3, Black starts a dangerous attack in spite of his limited material by 31..., KtxKtP; 32 QxKt, BxKt; 33 Q-Kt7, Q-K5 ch; 34 K-Kt1, Q-B6; and now if 35 Q-B6, RxB!?

31	...	B-B1!
32	Q-QB6	Q-K5 ch
33	K-Kt1	

If P-B3, the black squares become terribly weak.

| 33 | ... | Kt-K4 |
| 34 | Kt-B3 | |

The only hope!

34	...	Kt-B6 ch
35	K-R1	Q-K4
36	K-Kt2	Kt-R5 ch
37	K-Kt1	

| 37 | ... | B-Q3! |

With this move the black attack reaches its peak. The text-move involves an offer of the exchange because after 38 B-B4, Black has to play QxB. This was actually White's best chance, though after 39 QxR ch, K-Kt2; 40 R-Q1!, Q-R7 ch; 41 K-B1, QxRP ch; 42 K-K2, QxP ch; Black's K-side pawns must prove decisive.

| 38 | R-Q1 | Q-R7 ch |
| 39 | K-B1 | RxB! |

The exchange is still sacrificed!

Resigns

Because of 40 PxR, Q-Kt7 ch; 41 K-K1, Kt-B6 mate.

GAME 28

Benkő switches the opening onto unusual lines with his 6th move and then tries to surprise his opponent with a neat tactical turn on the 10th move. Thus we see Tal finding his way remarkably quickly through unfamiliar opening lines as well. Not he, but his opponent, gets confused and after another six moves he has a decisive advantage which he exploits with confident precision.

SICILIAN DEFENCE

TAL		BENKŐ
1	P-K4	P-QB4
2	Kt-KB3	Kt-QB3
3	P-Q4	PxP
4	KtxP	Kt-B3
5	Kt-QB3	P-KKt3

A move that used to be fashionable fifty years ago, its idea being that Black might be able to play P-Q4 in a single move, since that move was regarded as an equalizing move in the Dragon variation. Later the omission of 5..., P-Q3; was thought to be risky, because after 5..., P-KKt3; 6 KtxKt, KtPxKt; 7 P-K5, White held some advantage. However, in that line Black can play 6..., QPxKt; QxQ ch, KxQ; with an end-game which it is by no means certain White can claim to be advantageous to him, although he has chances after 8 B-KB4, and 9 0-0-0. Tal, however, goes his own way with a move more suited to his style and one likely to create middle game complications.

| 6 | B-QB4 | Q-R4 |

After 6..., B-Kt2; 7 KtxKt, is strong, so Benkő not unnaturally looks for a different idea, though the game is hardly a recommendation for the one selected.

| 7 | 0-0 | B-Kt2 |

After 7..., Q-QB4; 8 KtxKt, QxB; 9 Kt-K5, Q-B2; 10 Kt-Q3, White has suffi-

cient pressure in the centre to compensate him for the loss of the two bishops.

8	Kt–Kt3	Q–B2
9	B–KKt5	o–o
10	P–B4!	

Black is already in difficulties, faced as he is with the two threats of BxKt followed by Kt–Q5 and alternatively P–K5. If now 10 . . ., P–Q3; he only blocks the latter threat and after 11 BxKt, BxB; 12 Kt–Q5, and 13 KtxB ch, he has a ruined pawn skeleton. His attempt to escape the dilemma is interesting.

10	...	P–Kt4

A conception borrowed from the Benoni Defence. If 11 BxP, he wins the KP by 11 . . ., Q–Kt3 ch; 12 K–R1, KtxP. Although Tal energetically repudiates the move, Benkő can hardly be blamed for trying it. The error is not here but earlier. Assuming that Black has nothing better than the move chosen on his 6th move, then 5 . . ., P–KKt3; can be said to be the source of the trouble.

11	BxKt!	KtPxB
12	Kt–Q5	Q–Kt1
13	BxB	KxB
14	Kt–Q4	P–K3?

After this his position becomes hopeless. True, he could not play 14 . . ., QxKtP; 15 KtxKt, PxKt; 16 R–Kt1, because after 17

Kt–B7, he will lose the exchange, but 14 . . ., Q–Q3; was better, though even then White gets an advantage after 15 P–B3, or 15 Kt–K3.

15	KtxKt	QPxKt

16	Q–Q4 ch!

Had Black's Q been on Q3, this could not have been played, since 16 . . ., P–B3; would win the knight owing to the pin. Now White wins a pawn in addition to having the better position.

16	...	P–B3
17	Kt–K3	Q–Kt3
18	QxQ	PxQ
19	KtxP	P–QKt4

19 . . ., B–R3; 20 KtxP, is even worse.

20	Kt–Q6	P–K4

Otherwise White plays P–K5.

21	PxP	PxP
22	RxR	KxR
23	KtxB	RxKt

(See first diagram on next page.)

Rook endings with a difference of only one pawn often end in a draw. But now we see Tal's faultless technique as an end-game player.

24	P–QR4!	PxP
25	RxP	R–Q1

To accept a passive role for his rook would be to admit defeat.

| 26 | R–B4 | R–Q3 |
| 27 | R–B5 | R–K3 |

But he is forced into a passive position after all.

28	P–QKt4	K–K2
29	P–B4	K–Q2
30	K–B2	R–K1
31	K–K3	R–QKt1

Making another vain attempt to activate the rook.

32	P–Kt5	PxP
33	PxP	K–Q3
34	R–Q5 ch	K–K3

The king cannot get at the passed pawn owing to the need to defend his own KP. It is just one more nail in his coffin.

| 35 | K–Q3 | R–Kt2 |

35 ..., R–QB1; 36 P–Kt6, R–QKt1; 37 R–Kt5, K–Q3; 38 K–B4, leads nowhere.

36	K–B4	R–Kt1
37	R–B5!	K–Q3
38	R–B6 ch	K–Q2
39	K–B5	R–KB1

A last attempt to get active play for his rook.

| 40 | P–Kt6 | R–B7 |

| 41 | R–B7 ch | K–K3 |

If 41 ..., K–Q1; 42 K–Q6, RxP; 43 RxP, White wins.

42	P–Kt7	R–B7 ch
43	K–Kt6	R–Kt7 ch
44	K–R7	R–R7 ch
45	K–Kt8	RxP
46	K–B8	R–Kt7
47	RxP	K–B3
48	P–R4!	

Destroying Black's last hope, such as it was.

48	...	P–Kt4
49	PxP ch	KxP
50	R–KB7	Resigns

GAME 29

Only an extraordinarily acute appreciation of position could lead Tal to sacrifice a piece as astonishingly as he does against Füster. A pawn capture away from the centre had already given an indication that he was in an original mood. The sacrifice is one of those whose consequences cannot be foreseen beyond the fact that a complicated position with tactical opportunities will result. As so often in such situations, Tal's opponent fails to find the way out and Füster's position here collapses in a mere ten moves. The game is flavoured with the true essence of Tal.

CARO-KANN DEFENCE

	TAL	FÜSTER
1	P–K4	P–QB3
2	P–Q4	P–Q4
3	Kt–QB3	PxP
4	KtxP	Kt–Q2

Theory regards this variation as entirely adequate.

| 5 | Kt–KB3 | |

Possibly 5 B–QB4, is stronger because of the line 5 . . . , KKt–B3; 6 Kt–Kt5, P–K3; 7 Q–K2, Kt–Kt3 (not P–KR3?; 8 KtxBP!); 8 B–Kt3, and now 8 . . . , QxP; is proved inadequate by 9 KKt–B3, and 10 Kt–K5.

| 5 | . . . | KKt–B3 |
| 6 | KtxKt ch | |

After 6 Kt–Kt3, P–K3; 7 B–Q3, B–K2; 8 o–o, o–o; Black has a constricted but solid position.

| 6 | . . . | KtxKt |
| 7 | B–QB4 | |

Preventing B–Kt5, which would be answered by BxP ch and Kt–K5 ch.

| 7 | . . . | B–B4 |

For some time the fashion was to play P–KKt3 here, to which 8 Kt–Kt5, is probably the best answer.

8	Q–K2	P–K3
9	B–KKt5	B–K2
10	o–o–o	P–KR3

White has developed his game so that if Black castles here, he can start an attack by Kt–K5, P–KKt4 and P–KR4. Kt–K5 would moreover be a deterrent to Q-side castling by Black. The best chance for Black to equalize here was 10 . . . , Kt–Q4. Instead, he takes a preliminary precaution which turns sour on him.

| 11 | B–R4! | |

Black would have good play after 11 BxKt, BxB; 12 P–Q5, Q–Kt3.

| 11 | . . . | Kt–K5 |

Revealing the intention behind his previous move, the elimination of the white QB. Nevertheless, the less ambitious 11 . . . , Kt–Q4; 12 B–KKt3, o–o; would have been better though still not easy for him, because against the text-move White has an interesting tactical device.

| 12 | P–KKt4! | |

Tal never misses a trick like this! Now if 12 . . . , BxB; then 13 PxB, KtxP; 14 PxP, with a very dangerous attack.

| 12 | . . . | B–R2 |
| 13 | B–KKt3! | KtxB |

| 14 | BPxKt! | |

White is certainly not bound by the dogma that all captures should be towards the centre. The move was no doubt a surprise to Black, though it is essentially logical since the KB file is more important than the KR file. Pressure on Black's KB2 will now deter Q-side castling, while castling on the K side can be met with a pawn storm. Black's position is not much eased now by 14 . . . , B–Q3; 15 B–Kt3, Q–R4, 16 Kt–K5.

| 14 | . . . | Q–B2 |
| 15 | Kt–K5 | B–Q3 |

In order to defend his KB2 he might have tried R–KB1 and B–Kt3.

16	P–KR4	P–B3?

Since castling on either side at the moment is too hazardous, he aims to continue with 17 Kt–B3, 0–0–0; 18 BxP ch, K–Kt1; giving up a pawn which he may well recapture once his king is safe. However, White refutes the text-move with a most unexpected sacrifice which keeps the black king in the centre, and therefore Black's best line was to play 16..., BxKt; 17 PxB, R–Q1; with good chances of resistance.

17 BxP!

A typical Tal sacrifice, which cannot be refused and which ensures that the black king remains in the centre and under fire along the Q file and KB file. There is no doubt that many of the ensuing possibilities were foreseen by Tal at this point.

17	...	PxKt
18	PxP	B–K2

Not BxKP; 19 KR–K1, recovering the piece with a powerful attack.

19 KR–B1!

If 19 B–Q7 ch, Black could have blunted the attack by QxB and had fair compensation. White prefers to retain the tension and now threatens 20 B–B7 ch, K–B1; 21 B–Kt6 dis. ch, K–Kt1; 22 Q–B4 ch.

19	...	R–KB1

20	RxR ch	BxR
21	Q–B3!	

Only three pieces left, but plenty for Tal! This prevents 21..., R–Q1; because after 22 RxR ch, mate follows. If Black tries to free his game by 21..., B–Kt3; then 22 P–R5, B–B2; 23 R–Q7, winning. So Black tries to shift the objectionable bishop, or even to sacrifice the queen for two pieces.

21	...	Q–K2
22	Q–Kt3!	

Better than trying for an advantageous ending by 22 B–Q7 ch, QxB; 23 RxQ, KxR, 24 Q–B7 ch, B–K2; 25 QxP. Now the possibility is still on with the queen coming in at QKt7 instead on KB7, and also if 22..., R–Q1; he wins the queen by 23 B–B7 ch.

22	...	R–Kt1?

Losing quickly. Better was 22..., P–QKt4; 23 B–Q7 ch, QxB; 24 RxQ, KxR; 25 Q–B7 ch, B–K2; 26 QxP, B–K5; 27 QxP, and White's passed pawns must decide the issue.

23	B–Q7 ch	QxB
24	RxQ	KxR
25	Q–B7 ch	B–K2
26	P–K6 ch	K–Q1

Naturally if 26..., K–Q3; 27 Q–B4 ch, and wins the rook.

27 QxP   Resigns

For after 27..., B–K5; 28 Q–K5, winning
a piece.

GAME 30

Petrosian, many times lightning chess
champion of the Soviet Union, reckoned
that Tal was a second a move quicker than
he, so Tal was indeed a man of quick
decisions. In the following game he at once
spotted Larsen's one mistake, right at the
start of the complications and the punish-
ment he meted out was not only severe but
a demonstration of fine technical polish.

SICILIAN DEFENCE

	TAL	LARSEN
1	P–K4	P–QB4
2	Kt–KB3	P–Q3
3	P–Q4	PxP
4	KtxP	Kt–KB3
5	Kt–QB3	P–QR3
6	B–KKt5	QKt–Q2

Aiming to develop an early action on the
Q side, but the move has the disadvantage
that it does nothing to disturb the strong
knight on White's Q4.

7   B–QB4

Very strong since the bishop develops great
activity on this diagonal, even though it
seems directly to invite Black to continue
his attack on the Q side and against the
KP. The bishop derives its dynamic force
largely from the knight on Q4, and the
following miniature, won by Nejmetdinov
in 1951, shows what can happen: 7...,
P–K3; 8 o–o, P–Kt4?; 9 BxKP, PxB; 10
KtxKP, Q–Kt3; 11 Kt–Q5, KtxKt; 12
QxKt, B–Kt2; 13 Kt–B7 ch, and mates in
two. Nor in that variation is 8..., Q–B2;
much better for then 9 BxKP, PxB; 10
KtxP, Q–B5; 11 Kt–Q5!, with a strong
attack (Keres–Shaitar, Amsterdam Olympics, 1954). So this consideration must

always be in the forefront of Black's cal-
culations.

7 ...   Q–R4

A Russian invention. Another way to avoid
the bishop sacrifice is 7..., P–R3; 8 B–R4,
P–K3; 9 o–o, Kt–B4; but after 10 R–K1,
White has the better game (Nejmetdinov–
Shamkovich, 1954).

8   Q–Q2   P–K3
9   o–o

9 o–o–o, P–Kt4; 10 B–Kt3, used to be
played. Here 10 BxKP, is not effective
because after 10..., PxB; 11 KtxKP,
K–B2; 12 KtxB, RxKt; 13 QxP, P–Kt5; 14
Kt–Q5, QxP; White's king is in trouble.
Castling on the other side is now preferred
because after 9..., P–Kt4; 10 B–Q5!,
PxB; 11 Kt–B6!, Q–Kt3; 12 PxP, White
obtains a strong attack on the king in the
centre.

9   ...   P–R3
10   B–R4   B–K2
11   QR–Q1   Kt–K4

The natural-looking 11..., o–o; is met by
12 Kt–Q5!

12   B–QKt3

The retreat to K2 was also worth considering.

12   ...   P–KKt4

Securing the position of his knight on K4.

13   B–Kt3   B–Q2

Better chances are offered by 13...,
Kt–R4. The game Tal–Korchnoi in the
XXVIth Championship then continued 14
B–R4 ch, P–Kt4; 15 BxKt, PxQB; 16
Kt–B6. Q–B2; 17 KtxB, KxKt!; 18 B–Kt3,
and White has only a minimal advantage.

14   P–B4!   PxP
15   BxBP   Kt–R4

Q–B2 would be more prudent.

| 16 | BxKt | QxB |

If 16..., PxB; White develops dangerous threats by 17 Kt-B5, B-B4 ch; 18 K-R1, 0-0-0: 19 Kt-Q6 ch, BxKt; 20 QxB, B-B3; 21 Q-K7.

17	K-R1	Kt-B3
18	Kt-B3	Q-KR4
19	P-K5!	PxP

20 Kt-K4!

White exploits the opening of the K file with great energy, recognizing that Black's next, apparently natural, move is a decisive mistake.

20 ... 0-0-0?

Leading to a forced loss. Even after the preferable 20..., B-B3; 21 Kt-Kt3, Q-Kt5; 22 KtxP, Q-Kt4; 23 Q-K2, Black's position remains difficult.

21	Kt-Kt3	Q-Kt5
22	KtxP	Q-KR5
23	Q-B3 ch	K-Kt1
24	KtxB ch	Resigns

For if 24..., KtxKt; 25 RxKt, winning a piece owing to the undefended position of the black KR.

GAME 31

Tal, who for once selects a close opening, soon outwits his opponent, and by the 15th move de Grieff is already lost. However,

Tal made one superficial move and gave Black a chance to save himself. When this was not taken, the greater force of the white pieces soon decided the issue. In spite of the one doubtful move, the game is still one of high quality.

ENGLISH OPENING

	TAL	DE GRIEFF
1	P-QB4	Kt-KB3
2	Kt-QB3	P-K3
3	Kt-B3	P-Q4
4	P-K3	B-K2
5	P-QKt3	0-0
6	B-Kt2	P-QKt3

P-B4 with freer play in the centre is probably better, but at this point it is largely a matter of taste. Black gives the impression both here and later that respect for his great opponent is making him unduly prudent, though excessive prudence is often the greater risk.

7	P-Q4	B-Kt2
8	B-Q3	QKt-Q2
9	0-0	Kt-K5

Continuing to omit the move P-B4, which is essential to this variation.

10	PxP	PxP
11	Q-K2	P-QR3
12	Q-B2	

Not as inconsequent as it looks. By threatening 12 B-R6, he has induced Black to weaken his Q side.

12	...	P-KB4
13	Kt-K2	B-Q3
14	Kt-K5	

Strategically outwitting his opponent. He threatens P-B3, and after the knight retreats, he has a double attack on the black KBP. Black's hope is therefore to force P-B4 at once by an attack on the white knight, but then the position of White's knight is reinforced.

| 14 | ... | Q-K2 |

The new world champion, with M. Marcel Berman, president of the F. I. D. E.

The correct plan, but the wrong method. Correct was 14 ..., Q–K1; so that after 15 QR–B1, R–B1; 16 Kt–B6, he can continue 16 ..., Kt–Kt1.

15 QR–B1   QR–B1

He has reached a lost position without a fight! There was a little more chance in 15 ..., P–B4; 16 KtxKt, QxKt; 17 P–B3, Kt–Kt4; 18 P–KR4, Kt–B2; 19 BxBP, Q–K2; 20 BxP ch, K–R1; 21 PxP, BxP; though he has no compensation whatever for his lost material.

16 Kt–B6   Q–R5
17 Kt–B4   Kt(Q2)–B3

An uncommon situation! Black is hamstrung by the white knights, but if he uses the bishops to take them off, his position becomes quite hopeless.

18 P–Kt3   Q–R3
19 P–B3   P–KKt4
20 KtxP   KtxKt
21 PxKt   PxP

KtxP would allow 22 B–B4 ch. White is now ready to reap the benefit of his excellent play. The black king is exposed, while the black queen and queen's bishop are out of play.

22 BxP?

Superficial play, for after 22 ..., RxR ch; 23 RxR, KtxP; White has no win. Correct was 22 RxR ch, first and only then 23 BxP.

22 ...   KtxP?

Quid pro quo.

23 RxR ch   RxR
24 Q–K2   BxKt
25 BxB   P–Kt5
26 P–QR3   Q–Kt4

27 R–K1

Forcing the knight away. The opening of the K file ends the game.

27 ...   Kt–B4
28 Q–K6 ch   R–B2
29 B–Q5   Resigns

GOLD MEDAL AT THE WORLD TEAM CHAMPIONSHIP AT MUNICH

The 13th World Team Tournament took place at Munich in the autumn of 1958 and the Soviet Union entered a most powerful team, with Mikhail Tal's name on the entry list as no more than a reserve. But the reserve player, winning game after game on the fourth board, became the highest point scorer, not only in the Soviet team but in the whole tournament. He had a 90 per cent score, obtaining 13½ points out of 15 without defeat. As a member of the winning team, he became the owner of an Olympic gold medal. The chess Olympics are a severe test of endurance owing to their intensely crowded programme. Tal took this in his stride, his peculiar qualities proving ideal in such a situation. In his series of victories he used up only a small part of the time on his clock, and in so compressed a programme this feature of his play proved to be one against which there was no antidote.

GAME 32

Everything in the right place is a rule well exemplified in Tal's next game. With a neat blending of strategy and tactics he gains time to prepare a K-side attack by threatening the KP on move 14. With an exchange of rooks Darga halts the attack on his king but in the process weakens his pawn structure. Tal then breaks up the pawns winning one of them and quickly finishes off the game in a Q ending.

RUY LOPEZ

	TAL	DARGA
1	P-K4	P-K4
2	Kt-KB3	Kt-QB3
3	B-Kt5	P-QR3
4	B-R4	Kt-B3
5	O-O	B-K2
6	R-K1	P-QKt4
7	B-Kt3	P-Q3
8	P-B3	O-O
9	P-KR3	Kt-Q2
10	P-Q4	Kt-Kt3
11	B-K3	R-Kt1

Black's system of defence occurred in the Tal–Panno game, where 11 ..., PxP; was played with the continuation 12 PxP, Kt-R4; 13 B-B2, P-QB4. Darga's move is too artificial to be an improvement. The idea is that after Kt-B5 his rook will be on an open file if White takes the knight, but such moves are only good when the intended line cannot be avoided by the opponent without disadvantage. Otherwise, as here, they simply lose time. White at once turns the game into a different channel by developing an attack on the black KP.

12	PxP!	KtxP
13	KtxKt	PxKt

14	Q-R5!	Q-Q3
15	Kt-Q2	B-B3
16	Kt-B3	Kt-B5
17	QR-Q1	Q-K2
18	B-Kt5!	

The attack on the KP has given White time to build up an attack on the king. Had White been forced to play 18 B-B1 here, so as to defend his QKtP, Black would have had nothing to worry about. But now if 18..., KtxP; 19 BxB, QxB; 20 R-Q2, Kt-B5; 21 BxKt, PxB; 22 QxKP, White recovers his pawn with advantage owing to Black's damaged pawn skeleton. Even in this variation the rook on Black's QKt1 serves no useful purpose.

18	...	P-Kt3
19	BxB	QxB
20	Q-R6	Q-K2

If Q-Kt2, White leads into an advantageous ending by 21 QxQ ch, KxQ; 22 R-K2, P-KB3; 23 Kt-K1, with Kt-Q3-B5 to follow.

| 21 | R-Q3! | P-KB3 |

Now if KtxP; 22 Kt-Kt5. He stops that threat but only at the cost of a severe weakening of his pawn structure.

22	Kt-R4	P-Kt4
23	Kt-B5	BxKt
24	PxB	K-R1

Unpinning the knight looks reasonable enough, but after the rooks are exchanged there is a threat of mate by Q-B8. A line worth considering was 24..., QR-Q1; 25 R(K1)-Q1, RxR; 26 RxR, R-Q1; 27 RxR ch, QxR; 28 P-KR4, Q-Q7; since White gets nowhere by 29 BxKt, PxB; 30 PxP, owing to 30..., Q-B8 ch; 31 K-R2, Q-B5 ch.

25	R(K1)-Q1	KR-Q1
26	RxR ch	RxR
27	RxR ch	QxR

| 28 | P-KR4! | |

Now this is very strong, since 28..., Q-Q7; would be answered by 29 Q-B8 mate. Black must defend his KKtP.

28	...	P-KKt5
29	BxKt	PxB
30	K-R2!	K-Kt1
31	Q-R5!	Q-Q7

He cannot avoid the loss of a pawn, for if 31..., Q-Q8; 32 Q-K8 ch, wins the KBP, nor has Black any hope of perpetual check.

32	QxKtP ch	K-B1
33	P-B3!	QxKtP
34	QxP	Q-KB7

35   K–R3!   Resigns

He loses more material, and if he tries for perpetual check by Q–Kt8, Tal simply plays 36 QxBP, P–KR4; 37 Q–Q8 ch, and 38 Q–Q2.

GAME 33

Walther with the white pieces played to get a close game but only succeeded for a very short time. His 10th move looked as if it fitted in with his plan, but Tal immediately observed its drawbacks and fell upon his opponent with unbounded ferocity. Complications at once resulted and Tal very soon held an advantage which he maintained with a series of witty tactical manoeuvres and indeed increased up to a point where he could force the mate.

SICILIAN DEFENCE

	WALTHER	TAL
1	P–K4	P–QB4
2	Kt–K2	Kt–KB3
3	P–Q3	Kt–B3
4	Kt–Q2	P–Q4
5	P–QB3	PxP
6	PxP	P–KKt3
7	Q–B2	B–Kt2
8	P–QR4	

The natural preparation for Kt–QB4.

8   ...   0–0
9   Kt–QB4   Kt–QR4!
10   Kt–B4?

Although this move must be queried, its fault is by no means obvious.

10   P–K4!

Driving the knight where it wants to go anyway and weakening the square it wants to occupy! Of a similar move Dr. Tarrasch once wrote that it could only be played by a rabbit or a genius. Here it is explained by a combinative turn. 11 KtxKP, is no good because of 11 ..., R–K1.

11   Kt–Q5   KtxP!
12   QxKt

Or 12 KtxKt, QxKt(Q4); 13 B–QB4, Q–Q1; 14 QxKt, QxKt.

12   ...   Kt–Kt6
13   R–R3

Naturally not 13 R–Kt1, B–B4.

13   ...   B–B4
14   Q–K3   KtxB
15   QxBP

No better is 15 QxKt, QxKt; 16 Kt–K3, Q–K5; 17 P–B3, Q–KB5!

15   ...   R–K1
16   Q–K3   B–KB1!
17   Kt–Kt4

If 17 P-QKt4, QxKt; 18 QxKt, P-QR4; 19 Q-Kt2, Q-K5 ch; 20 Kt-K3, PxP.

17	...	P-QR4
18	KtxRP	QxKt
19	QxKt	BxKt
20	PxB	QxP ch
21	R-B3	

If 21 Q-B3, Q-K5 ch; 22 Q-K3, Q-Kt8 ch.

| 21 | ... | Q-K5 ch |
| 22 | B-K2 | RxP |

The complications so far have not only cost White a pawn but have prevented his castling.

23	P-B3	Q-R5 ch!
24	P-Kt3	Q-QKt5
25	P-Kt4	

A violent and desperate effort to create chances in a lost position, but he merely gives Tal the opportunity of reverting to combinative play.

| 25 | .... | P-K5! |

An obvious move since after 25 PxB, PxP; he recovers the piece with advantage. Its attractiveness lies in the fact that Tal is going to leave the bishop en prise after White's reply.

26	P-B4	R-R7!
27	PxB	RxP
28	O-O	

Allowing Black to recover his piece and come out two pawns up. But against the threats of R-Kt8 and R-Kt6 the only alternative was 28 K-B2, and then 28.... P-K6 ch!; followed either by 29 RxP, QxP ch; or by 29 K-B3, Q-K5 ch.

28	...	RxB
29	R-B8	Q-Kt3 ch
30	K-R1	RxR
31	QxR ch	K-Kt2
32	PxP	RPxP
33	P-B5	Q-KB3!
34	QxP	Q-K4!
	Resigns	

GAME 34

Tal chooses an active defence against Lago's English Opening and with both players playing sharply there are open KB and KKt files after the 13th move. But whereas Black's initiative develops well on the KB file, the other file is no use to White. Tal wins a couple of pawns by some neat tactical turns and wins an ending where he is a pawn ahead in the simplest manner.

ENGLISH OPENING

	LAGO	TAL
1	P-QB4	P-K4
2	Kt-QB3	Kt-KB3
3	Kt-B3	P-Q3
4	P-KKt3	P-KKt3
5	B-Kt2	B-Kt2
6	P-Q3	O-O
7	B-Q2	Kt-R4
8	Q-B1	P-KB4
9	B-R6	Kt-QB3
10	BxB	KxB

White has spent four moves exchanging Black's KB, which helps him little in a position where his pieces are not placed for an attack on the king's wing. Black, who has made better use of the time, is now ready to take the initiative.

11	Kt–Q5	P–B5
12	Q–B3	B–K3
13	KtxKBP?	

The opening of the KB and KKt files which follows this move only help Black who finds a good target on White's KB2 whereas White has no such target on the KKt file. True, he gets a foothold on his KKt5 but Black does not even have to take any steps to counter him.

13	...	KtxKt
14	PxKt	RxP
15	P–KR4	Q–B3
16	Kt–Kt5?	

Attractive because he can answer 16 ..., RxBP; with 17 Kt–K4. But after Tal's neat and vigorous reply he gets the worst of it.

16 ...   Kt–Q5!

An unexpected turn, inviting a pawn fork and then after 17 ..., RxBP; 18 Kt–K4, again.

| 17 | P–K3 | RxBP! |
| 18 | PxKt | |

He sees that Kt–K4 is no good now because of 18 ..., R–K7 ch; 19 K–Q1, Q–B1!; 20 PxKt, RxB.

18 ...   B–Kt5!

A splendid move! If White now tries to save his bishop by 19 BxP, then 19 ..., R–K7 ch; 20 K–Q1, R–R7 dis. ch!; 21 K–B1, RxR ch; 22 BxR, Q–B8 ch; 23 K–B2 (not K–Q2, Q–K7 ch; 24 K–B1, Q–Q8 mate), QxR; coming out the exchange up since 24 BxR, is impossible because of Q–Q8 mate.

19	B–B3	RxB!
20	O–O–O	Q–B5 ch
21	K–Kt1	QxP!

He is actually simplifying! If now 22 KtxR, QxQ: 23 PxQ, BxKt.

| 22 | QxQ | PxQ |
| 23 | KR–Kt1 | |

23 ...   R–Kt6!

Another neat tactical turn which forces the exchange of one pair of rooks. White recovers a pawn but he cannot hold his KRP and then the passed K-side pawns must win.

24	RxR	BxR
25	K–B1	B–R4
26	Kt–K6 ch	K–R3
27	KtxBP	

At least Black is going to have two weak queen's pawns.

| 27 | ... | R–KB1 |
| 28 | Kt–K6 | R–B8 ch |

29	K–B2	R–B7 ch
30	K–B1	P–R3
31	Kt–Kt5	

31 KtxP, is just as useless since the KRP is untenable.

| 31 | ... | R–B5 |
| 32 | Kt–K4 | |

| 32 | ... | B–B6! |

A perfect piece of end-game technique. When the knight moves, the bishop will be defending the QKtP, thus preventing White from obtaining a passed QBP. There is no hurry to take the KRP.

33	KtxP	K–R4
34	R–Kt5 ch	KxP
35	R–K5	P–KR4
36	P–B5	P–KKt4
37	Kt–B5 ch	RxKt!

The simplest way.

38	RxR	K–Kt5
39	R–B8	P–R5
40	R–Q8	P–R6
41	RxP ch	K–Kt6
	Resigns	

GAME 35

Though the styles of play of Capablanca and Tal are extreme opposites, the former seeking simplicity and the latter complexity,
they have one factor in common and that is an almost phenomenal elegance. There is a story that Capablanca, having made his move in a tournament game, strolled round the room. He looked at the position in another game and whispered to a spectator what he considered the best move. Afterwards this particular move was only found by the analysts with the utmost difficulty. Tal equally considers the most difficult combinations with the greatest rapidity and hardly ever gets into time trouble. Unbelievable as it may seem, he selected the continuation stemming from the pawn sacrifice on move 14 in the following game after no more than a few seconds' thought, and spent scarcely half an hour over the whole game.

SICILIAN DEFENCE

	BENI	TAL
1	P–K4	P–QB4
2	P–QB4	

Trying for a close game and at the same time to avoid the "book." The move, however, unnecessarily weakens his Q4 and gives Tal the chance of seizing an early initiative.

2	...	Kt–QB3
3	Kt–QB3	Kt–B3
4	P–Q3	

He clearly has no intention of trying to play the usual P–Q4, unlike his opponent who gets the move in as quickly as possible.

4	...	P–K3
5	P–B4	P–Q4
6	P–K5	Kt–KKt1

This is not to be reckoned as loss of time, since he has induced White to change his pawn structure and can now aim the knight at KB4.

| 7 | Kt–B3 | Kt–K2 |
| 8 | B–K2 | Kt–B4 |

9	0-0	B-K2
10	Q-K1	0-0
11	Kt-Q1	

Black already has an advantage in that his pieces are poised for action while White is having to indulge in awkward regrouping. Tal now opens the Q file and starts to use direct tactical threats.

11	. . .	PxP!
12	PxP	Kt-Kt5!
13	Q-B3	Kt-Q5!
14	B-Q3	

14 KtxKt, PxKt; 15 Q-Q2 (Q-QKt3, P-Q6; 16 B-B3, P-Q7), P-Q6; 16 B-B3, Q-Q5 ch; 17 Kt-K3, Kt-B7; 18 R-Kt1, B-B4; would be favourable to Black. Black's natural answer to the text-move is 14 ..., P-QKt3; but Tal chooses a more complicated and risky line, involving a pawn sacrifice, and selects it moreover almost instantaneously.

| 14 | . . . | P-QKt4! |

Giving the game a typical Tal twist.

15	PxP	B-Kt2
16	B-B4	Kt-Q4
17	Q-Q2	Kt-Kt3

Black is now calling the tune.

18	B-K2	Q-B2
19	KtxKt	

Closing the Q file at least. But now the passed pawn becomes strong and it is instructive to see how Tal increases his positional advantage.

19	. . .	PxKt
20	B-Q3	Kt-Q4
21	P-QR3	

| 21 | . . . | P-QR3! |

The opening of the QR file will increase Black's advantage.

22 Q-K2

There is no help in 22 PxP, QBxP; 23 BxB, RxB; because of the following continuations: I. 24 K-R1, Q-B5; and 25 ..., KR-B1. II. 24 Q-Q3 (or K2), Kt-Kt5! III. 24 Kt-B2, Kt-K6.

22	. . .	PxP
23	BxP	Q-Kt3
24	K-R1	Kt-Kt5
25	P-QR4	

If 25 Kt-B2, then 25 ..., KR-B1; and 26 ..., R-B7.

25	. . .	P-Q6!
26	Q-Kt4	

Not 26 BxP, KtxB; 27 QxKt, R-R3. So White goes in for a counter-demonstration, but it has no weight in it.

26	. . .	Kt–B7
27	R–QKt1	KR–Q1
28	B–Q2	Q–Q5
29	B–B3	Q–Q4
30	R–B3	P–Q7
31	P–B5	PxP
32	QxP	Kt–K8

Black's great positional advantage is obvious. As there is no chance of an endgame, the passed white pawns are of no value. Black's last move starts a decisive attack on the king and especially on KKt7. If White now tries 33 Kt–K3, Black can play 33 . . ., QxR!; 34 PxQ, KtxP!; and the following interesting variations all win for Black: I. 35 Q–B4, Kt–Kt4 dis. ch; 36 Kt–Kt2, P–Q8 = Q ch; 37 RxQ, RxR ch; 38 B–B1, Kt–R6; 39 Q–B5, P–Kt3! II. 35 Q–R3, B–B4! III. 35 Q–R5, P–Kt3; 36 Q–R3, B–B4!

33	R–Kt3	KtxP
34	K–Kt1	B–B4 ch
35	K–B1	

| 35 | . . . | Kt–B5! |

The coup de grace! White's final throw is already discounted.

36	RxP ch	K–B1
37	QxKt	Q–R8 ch
38	K–K2	Q–K8 mate

The passed pawn plays its part at last!

GAME 36

Tal's game against Milev cannot but impress. Milev dawdled over his development and his king got left in the centre. As in his game against Füster, Tal consolidated this situation with a remarkably deep piece sacrifice and then hustled his opponent to his doom in only twenty moves.

TARRASCH DEFENCE

	TAL	MILEV
1	P–QB4	P–QB4
2	Kt–QB3	Kt–QB3
3	Kt–B3	Kt–B3
4	P–K3	P–K3
5	P–Q4	P–Q4

A solid version of the Tarrasch Defence which can be traced right back to the days of Staunton. It is a variation with a great deal of hidden tension, which is all that Tal asks of an opening, a phase of the game in which he rarely tries to disprove his opponent's play.

6	PxQP	KKtxP
7	B–B4	

The analysts are still divided between the merits of this and 7 B–Q3.

| 7 | . . . | Kt–Kt3? |

Neglecting his development in an attempt to get out of the book.

8	B–Kt5	P–QR3?
9	BxKt ch	PxB
10	O–O	B–Kt2

11 Kt–K4!

From now every move of White's becomes a threat and Black has no time to castle.

11	...	Kt–Q2
12	Q–B2	Q–Kt3
13	Kt–K5!	

The positional move 13 B–Q2, was also strong, but Tal chose the text without hesitation.

13	...	PxP?

13 ..., KtxKt; 14 PxKt, might have been slightly better, though his game would still have been untenable owing to the weakness of the doubled QBP and of the square Q3. Milev, however, could hardly see how much more trouble he was going to be caused by the move chosen.

14	KtxKt	KxKt
15	PxP	K–K1
16	B–K3	Q–B2
17	P–Q5!	

The break-in by this and the next move is remarkable even among Tal's range of combinations.

17	...	KPxP

18 KR–K1!

There are two pieces blocking the rook's control of the file and one of them is attacked, yet in spite of that the occupation of the file quickly decides the issue. Black can hardly play 18 ..., PxKt; because of 19 QxKP ch, Q–K2; 20 Q–Q3!, R–Q1; 21 Q–Kt3, or if 19 ..., B–K2; 20 B–B5, and wins.

18	...	K–Q1
19	Q–Kt3	P–QB4

Tal's handling of the game has completely shattered Milev's morale, otherwise he would at least have tried 19 ..., K–B1; which promised a longer resistance.

20	KtxP	Resigns

GAME 37

Tal could have won the following game just as easily if it had occurred in a simultaneous display. Black's decisive mistake was made as early as the 6th move.

SCOTCH GAMBIT

	TAL	RUSSELL
1	P–K4	P–K4
2	Kt–KB3	Kt–QB3
3	P–Q4	PxP
4	P–B3	PxP
5	KtxP	P–Q3

The modern and more active continuation is 5 . . ., B-Kt5, but the old-fashioned line is sound enough.

6　B-QB4　　　B-K2?

This is where Black makes his mistake, after which he is at once under a grave disadvantage. Correct was 6 . . ., B-K3; 7 BxB, PxB; 8 Q-Kt3, Q-B1; 9 Kt-KKt5, Kt-Q1; and now White has a job to prove the soundness of his pawn sacrifice, the best continuation, according to Lasker, being 10 P-K5!

7	Q-Kt3	Kt-R4
8	BxP ch	K-B1
9	Q-R4	KxB
10	QxKt	

Two bishops are no compensation to Black for his having the poorer development, loss of the centre and inability to castle.

10	. . .	B-K3
11	O-O	K-B1

12　Kt-Q5!

A winning move already!

12　. . .　　　P-B3

Hoping that the knight will be subject to an awkward pin if it goes to QB7, but Tal solves this little problem with his usual elegance. Nor was 12 . . ., BxKt; 13 PxB,

much good because of the weakness of the white squares which will allow White a decisive attack before Black can get his king away by artificial castling. Probably best was 12 . . ., P-QKt3; though Black is lost anyway.

13　Kt-B7　　　B-B2

Equally if 13 . . ., B-Q2; 14 Kt-Q4, K-B2; 15 Q-R5 ch, P-Kt3; 16 Q-B3 ch, and wins.

14	Kt-Q4	Q-B1
15	KtxR	QxKt
16	Kt-B5	P-QKt3
17	Q-B3	B-B3
18	Q-KKt3	Kt-K2
19	QxP	K-K1
20	B-R6	R-Kt1
21	QR-Q1	Q-B1

22	BxP	KtxKt
23	PxKt	B-K2
24	KR-K1	B-K3
25	RxB	RxB
26	P-B6	Resigns

Quite a sparkling little ending.

GAME 38

Tal's game with Golombek was excellently contrived, and exemplified his diverse genius. First he surprised his opponent with a rare move right at the start, then he exerted his influence over the whole width of the board, preventing castling first on one side then on the other, and finally he drove out the king with a grand sacrificial conception till he met his fate in mid-board.

CARO-KANN DEFENCE

	TAL	GOLOMBEK
1	P–K4	P–QB3
2	P–Q4	P–Q4
3	P–K5	

Not theoretically the strongest, but it poses problems which are less well known, and it is typical of Tal to accept a risk for the sake of complications.

3	...	B–B4
4	P–QB4	

Bogolyubov's move, which was also used by Alekhine. Alekhine considered 3 P–K5, to be playable only if White continues dynamically with the text. Now Black will only do himself a disservice by winning a pawn with 4..., BxKt; 5 RxB, Q–R4 ch; 6 B–Q2, QxP.

4	...	P–K3
5	Kt–QB3	PxP?

And Tal already reaps the benefit of his 3rd and 4th moves, since Black now misjudges the position. He hopes to exploit the backward QP, but Tal shows that the pawn is not weak as Black cannot successfully try an attack on it. Indeed, Black is the loser because he gives up the centre. Better would have been 5..., Kt–K2; and if 6 P–B5, P–QKt3.

6	BxP	Kt–K2
7	KKt–K2	Kt–Q2
8	o–o	Kt–QKt3
9	B–Kt3	Q–Q2
10	P–QR4!	

Warning Black not to castle on the queen's side, and after the next move he starts uttering similar threats on the other wing.

10	...	P–QR4
11	Kt–Kt3	B–Kt3
12	B–B2!	

Forestalling the development of any attack on his QP by Kt–B4. Now Black has to deploy his knight via Q4 which upsets the co-ordination of his pieces and leaves him with one knight disadvantageously placed on QKt3.

12	..	BxB
13	QxB	Kt(K2)–Q4

Faced with the difficult problem of whether to capture the QP or not, Black rightly decides against it. After 13... QxP; 14 B–K3, Q–QKt5 (Q–Q1; 12 Q–Kt3); 15 R–R3, Kt(K2)–Q4; 16 R–Kt3, KtxB; 17 PxKt, Q–B4; 18 Q–B2, with a winning position for White.

14	Kt(B3)–K4	

Avoiding a freeing exchange for Black and beginning to regroup for action on the K side. If now 14..., B–K2; he has either 15 B–Kt5, or 15 Kt–QB5.

14	...	Kt–Kt5
15	Q–K2	Kt(Kt3)–Q4

If 15..., QxP; then 16 B–K3, Q–Q1; 17 Q–Kt4, threatening 18 Kt–R5, would be strong.

16	P–B4	P–KKt3
17	R–R3	B–K2
18	B–Q2	Kt–B7
19	R–Q3	Kt(Q4)–Kt5
20	BxKt	KtxB
21	R(Q3)–Q1	R–Q1
22	K–R1!	

A good waiting move. The king is removed from possible disturbing checks, while Black in a constricted position cannot easily find a target. In such situations mistakes easily occur.

22 ...   P-R4?

Weakening the black squares still further and giving up all ideas of castling.

23 Kt-B6 ch!

Showing that Black is in range of his guns. It is quite delightful to watch how the combinative attack is forced through.

| 23 ... | BxKt |
| 24 PxB | K-B1 |

Not 24 ..., o-o; 25 KtxP.

| 25 Kt-K4 | P-R5? |

Relatively better was Kt-Q4.

| 26 Kt-B5 | Q-B1 |

27 P-B5!

Starting the mating attack which is beautifully carried out. The first objective is KKt7. which he occupies in five moves after a double piece sacrifice.

27 ...	KtPxP
28 Q-K3	P-Kt3
29 Q-Kt5	R-R2

| 30 R-B4! | PxKt |
| 31 RxRP! | |

The objective must now be attained.

31 ...	RxR
32 Q-Kt7 ch	K-K1
33 Q-Kt8 ch	K-Q2
34 QxP ch	K-Q3
35 Q-K7 ch	Resigns

It is mate by 35 ..., K-Q4; 36 QxBP ch, K-K5; 37 Q-K5.

GAME 39

In this game Tal does not create complications but after surprising his opponent with a valuable opening novelty reaches an end-game with weaknesses in his opponent's position. On the 20th move he wins a pawn and exploits his advantage with technically perfect end-game play.

KING'S INDIAN DEFENCE

BERTHOLDT	TAL
1 P-Q4	Kt-KB3
2 P-QB4	P-KKt3
3 Kt-QB3	B-Kt2
4 P-K4	P-Q3
5 B-K2	o-o
6 P-B4	P-B4
7 Kt-B3	PxP
8 KtxP	Kt-B3
9 B-K3	B-Kt5

A striking improvement on the older 9 . . . , Kt–KKt5.

10 KtxKt

Or 10 Kt–B3, after which 10 . . . , P–K4!; is Black's best reply (Uhlmann–Geller, Dresden, 1959).

10	. . .	BxB
11	KtxQ	BxQ
12	RxB	

An attempt to win a pawn would not turn out well. For example, I. KtxKtP, B–B7. Or II. KtxBP, B–Kt5; 13 Kt–KKt5. P–KR3!; 14 Kt–B3, BxKt; 15 PxB, KR–B1!; 16 P–K5, PxP; 17 PxP, Kt–Q2; 18 Kt–Q5, K–B2; 19 P–B4, RxP. Or again III. 12 KtxBP, RxKt; 13 RxB, Kt–Kt5; 14 K–K2, R–QB1. All these variations are good for Black.

| 12 | . . . | KRxKt |
| 13 | K–K2 | P–QR3 |

Preparing a Q-side attack by QR–B1 and after White's P–QKt3, P–QKt4 at a suitable moment.

| 14 | P–QR4 | QR–B1 |
| 15 | B–Kt6? | |

A poor move. P–QKt3 was better.

15	. . .	R–K1
16	P–QKt3	Kt–Q2
17	B–Q4	

| 17 | . . . | BxB |

Black wins a pawn by exploiting the position of the rook on Q5.

18	RxB	Kt–B4
19	R–QKt1	Kt–K3
20	R–Q2	KtxP ch
21	K–K3	Kt–K3
22	Kt–Q5	R–B4
23	R–R2	Kt–B2
24	KtxKt	RxKt
25	P–R5	R–B4
26	K–Q4	R(K1)–QB1
27	R–KB1	P–B4

Having blockaded White's Q-side pawns, Black begins to mobilize his K-side majority.

28	R–K1	P–K4 ch
29	K–K3	K–B2
30	R–KB1	K–K3
31	R–Q1	P–R4
32	K–Q3	R–Q1
33	K–K3	PxP
34	KxP	P–Q4 ch

This decides the game, for now Black's extra pawn makes its weight increasingly felt.

35	K–K3	R–Q2
36	R–QB1	PxP
37	PxP	R–Q5
38	R–R4	R–B2
39	R–Kt4	K–B4
40	R–B1 ch	R–B5
41	RxR ch	PxR ch
42	K–Q4	P–KKt4
43	R–Kt6	P–Kt5
44	R–R6	R–Q2 ch
45	K–B5	P–B6
46	PxP	PxP
47	RxP ch	K–Kt5
	Resigns	

GAME 40

Tal's combinative power and positional appreciation are as effective in defence as in attack. This is excellently shown in his game against Lokvenc. The latter sacrificed a piece under duress on the 13th move and against the resulting attack Tal defended himself with perfect calm for 24 moves while his material advantage increased to a rook. By the 36th move it was time for his counter-attack and the issue was then decided in no more than five moves.

SICILIAN DEFENCE

	LOKVENC	TAL
1	P–K4	P–QB4
2	Kt–KB3	P–Q3
3	P–Q4	PxP
4	KtxP	Kt–KB3
5	Kt–QB3	P–QR3
6	B–Kt5	QKt–Q2
7	B–QB4	Q–R4
8	Q–Q2	P–K3
9	0–0–0	

This move has now been largely superseded by 9 0–0, which is much safer since after the text-move Black can start an energetic action on the Q side.

9	...	P–Kt4
10	B–Kt3	B–Kt2

10 ..., P–Kt5; would be too precipitate because of 11 Kt–Q5!, PxKt (KtxP; 12 QxP); 12 Kt–B6, and 13 PxP.

11	P–B3	

Now P–Kt5 was a real threat. He could play 11 KR–K1, because then 11 ... P–Kt5; yields no advantage owing to 12 Kt–Q5, PxKt (KtxP; 13 KtxKP!), KtxQ, 14 Kt (Q5)–B7 ch); 13 PxP dis. ch, K–Q1; 14 Kt–B6 ch, BxKt; 15 PxB, Kt–K4; 16 Q–B4. Black's best reply would be 11 ..., R–B1!; threatening RxKt, and then White would still have to play P–B3.

11	...	B–K2
12	K–Kt1	P–Kt5

13	Kt–Q5	

The sacrifice is forced since if 13 Kt(B3)–K2, KtxP! Black is now very much on the defensive.

13	...	PxKt
14	Kt–B5	B–KB1
15	PxP	Q–Kt3
16	KR–K1 ch	K–Q1
17	R–K2	R–B1!

Now Black is able in effect to castle and with his king in safety he ensures the failure of White's attack.

18	R(Q1)–K1	K–B2
19	B–K3	Kt–B4
20	B–Q4	K–Kt1
21	Kt–K3	KtxB

22	RPxKt	Q-Kt4
23	Kt-B4	KtxP
24	B-B2	B-B3
25	Q-Q4	R-B2
26	B-Kt3	K-R1
27	B-B2	R-Kt1
28	Q-R4	Kt-B3
29	Q-B4	P-R3
30	R-Q2	Kt-Q4
31	RxKt	

A vain attempt to infuse new life Into his attack.

31	...	BxR
32	Kt-Kt6 ch	K-Kt2
33	Q-Q4	B-K3
34	Kt-B4	K-Kt1
35	KtxP	BxKt
36	QxB	Q-B3

His careful defence now starts to bear fruit and the counter-attack begins.

37	QxP ch	K-R1
38	Q-Q2	R(Kt1)-QB1
39	P-QB4	B-B4 ch
40	K-R2	R-Kt2
41	Q-R5	B-B7
	Resigns	

GAME 41

Tal is a past master at perceiving, creating and exploiting even the most minute advantage. In his game against Fichtl he was unable to escape a major simplifica-tion and Fichtl's game looked as though it could well be saved, for though his pawns on QKt3 and K5 were weak, he had a protected passed pawn. By exploiting the forces of Zugzwang, Tal led into a queen ending in which his extra pawn brought him the desired win.

SICILIAN DEFENCE

	FICHTL	TAL
1	P-K4	P-QB4
2	Kt-KB3	P-Q3
3	P-Q4	PxP
4	KtxP	Kt-KB3
5	Kt-QB3	P-QR3
6	B-Kt5	P-K3
7	P-B4	P-R3
8	B-R4	Q-Kt3
9	Kt-Kt3	

By no means the strongest. 9 Q-Q2, which is strong in some variations, has had the sting taken out of it by Black's interpolation of P-KR3. But White could play 9 R-QKt1, Kt-B3; 10 B-B2, with support for his Q4. Or there is 9 P-QR3, after which 9...., QxP?; loses against 10 Kt-QR4. Finally he could try 9 Q-Q3, leading to a very complicated position.

9	...	Q-K6 ch
10	B-K2	QxBP

Correct. If 10..., KtxP; 11 KtxKt, QxKt: 12 0-0, with a powerful attack.

11	B-Kt3	Q-K6
12	BxP	Kt-B
13	BxB	

Forced, since 13 R-KB1, with the intention of stepping up the attack, proves un-satisfactory after 13..., KtxP; 14 KtxKt, QxKt; 15 BxB, RxB; 16 K-B2, Kt-K4; and White has insufficient compensation for the pawn.

13	...	RxB
14	Q-Q2	

Better was 14 Q-Q3, QxQ; 15 PxQ, so as not to allow the KP to be isolated or to give the black knight a free post on his K4.

14	...	QxQ ch
15	KxQ	B-Q2
16	K-K3	0-0-0
17	QR-Q1	Kt-K4
18	P-KR3	B-B3
19	Kt-R5	K-B2
20	KtxB	KxKt

After the victory

21	RxR	RxR
22	R–Q1	RxR
23	KtxR	K–B4
24	P–B3	P–QR4

Starting a vigorous minority attack which results in White securing a protected passed pawn but having a weak pawn on QKt3.

25	P–QKt3	P–QKt4
26	P–R?	P–Kt5
27	BPxP ch	PxP
28	P–QR4	K–Kt3
29	Kt–Kt2	Kt(B3)–Q2
30	B–Kt5	Kt–B4
31	Kt–B4 ch	KtxKt
32	BxKt	Kt–Kt2

Beginning an instructive knight manoeuvre.

33	K–Q4	Kt–R4
34	P–K5	Kt–B3 ch
35	K–K4	K–B4
36	B–K2	Kt–Q5

Now the knight attacks the QKtP from the centre so that the bishop is tied to its defence. Then, with White's king becoming increasingly restricted, the K-side majority can start to move.

37	B–B4	P–R4
38	P–Kt4	PxP
39	PxP	P–Kt4
40	K–K3	Kt–B3

The shift of the knight to QR4 is not a sign of hesitation but the means of exploiting a position that has been changed by the last few moves. A Zugzwang theme makes its appearance.

41	K–K4	Kt–R4
42	K–Q3	

White can no longer prevent Black from getting a passed QKtP, but this is not dangerous immediately as he cannot counter-attack White's QRP. However, a good triangulation manoeuvre changes the situation in Black's favour.

42	...	K–B3
43	K–Q4	K–Kt3

Now White's next move is forced, since if 44 K–Q3, K–B4; wins a pawn. Thus Black has put himself in a position to attack the QRP.

44	K–K4	KtxB
45	PxKt	K–R4
46	P–B5	P–Kt6
47	K–Q3	KxP
48	P–B6	K–R6
49	P–B7	P–Kt7
50	K–B2	K–R7
51	P–B8=Q	P–Kt8=Q ch

The queen ending with an extra pawn is a sure, if slow, win.

52	K–Q2	Q–Kt7 ch
53	K–Q3	Q–Kt4 ch
54	K–Q2	Q–Q4 ch
55	K–B2	Q–K5 ch
56	K–Q2	Q–Kt7 ch

He could have played QxKP now as he does five moves later.

57	K–Q3	Q–Kt6 ch
58	K–B2	Q–Kt6 ch
59	K–Q2	Q–Q4 ch
60	K–B2	Q–K5 ch
61	K–Q2	QxKP

He is forced to give up the idea of taking a pawn with check.

62	Q–R6 ch	K–Kt6
63	Q–Kt7 ch	K–B5
64	QxP	Q–Q5 ch
65	K–K1	QxP
66	Q–B1 ch	K–Q5
67	Q–B2 ch	K–K5
68	Q–B2 ch	K–B5
69	K–B2	Q–B6 ch

70	K–Kt1	P–K4
71	K–R2	Q–Kt6 ch
72	K–R1	Q–K8 ch
73	K–R2	P–Kt5
74	Q–B4 ch	Q–K5
75	Q–B7 ch	K–K6
76	K–Kt1	Q–Q5
77	K–Kt2	Q–K5 ch
78	K–Kt1	Q–B6
79	Q–K6	Q–Q8 ch
80	K–Kt2	Q–K7 ch
81	K–Kt3	Q–B6 ch
82	K–R4	P–K5
83	Q–Kt6 ch	K–K7
84	Q–B7	P–K6
	Resigns	

THE XXVITH CHAMPIONSHIP OF THE U. S. S. R.

That the young master from Riga was the darling of the public was mentioned in our notes to an earlier Championship. Since then he reached grandmaster rank but still remained favourite with his many fans. Though the public invariably enjoy watching the downfall of an idol, and he was a likely winner of the XXVIth Championship, his popularity was in no way diminished. What is the secret of his attraction to the chess public? Observing his slender, dark-haired figure, one can sense the nervous tension in his every movement and see the joy of battle light up his eye. He has all the appearance of the revolutionary and his followers revel in the way he falls upon even the greatest of his rivals, hazarding all in his efforts to overthrow them.

If coming events cast their shadows before them, it is certain that his successes in the XXVIth Championship were the forerunners of greater things.

GAME 42

Bronstein was of the opinion that he had "solved" the secret of Tal's style: "He plays quickly because he does not like strategical innovations in the opening. He likes to select a practical opening so as to start a correct attack. In this way he conserves his energy." Bronstein is himself something of a revolutionary, having reached the highest rank through his own peculiar ideas and exceptional depth. The following game between the two men is a real joy to watch.

RUY LOPEZ

	TAL	BRONSTEIN
1	P–K4	P–K4
2	Kt–KB3	Kt–QB3
3	B–Kt5	P–QR3
4	B–R4	Kt–B3
5	0–0	B–K2

Bronstein has often played White against the Tchigorin Defence and confessed that he fancied playing it as Black here.

6	R–K1	P–QKt4
7	B–Kt3	P–Q3
8	P–B3	0–0
9	P–KR3	Kt–QR4
10	B–B2	P–B4
11	P–Q4	Kt–B3
12	QKt–Q2	Q–Kt3

Konstantinopolsky's idea. The aim is to put pressure on White's KB2 and on the centre so as to force White to commit himself, thus easing Black's defensive problem. The drawback of the move is that the queen finds herself rather removed from the defence against any K-side attack that White may succeed in organizing.

13	PxBP	PₓP
14	Kt–B1	B–K3
15	Kt–K3	QR–Q1

| 16 | Q–K2 | P–Kt3 |
| 17 | Kt–Kt5 | P–B5! |

This normal advance is here a token of great tension beneath the surface. White can now hardly play KtxB because of the heavy pressure which would develop against his KB2. Nor can he step up his attack by 18 Q–B3, because of 18 . . . , P–R3; 19 KtxB, PxKt; 20 Kt–Kt4, and it is Black whose chances are improved.

It is a characteristic of Tal's play that he co-ordinates operations over the whole of the board and in his present dilemma this characteristic again asserts itself.

18	P–QR4!	K–Kt2!
19	PxP	PxP
20	R–Kt1	

Tal showed in subsequent analysis that this move, which was played relatively quickly, is in fact based on profound positional considerations. The more obvious 20 P–QKt3, would have led to 20 . . . , PxP; 21 KtxB ch, PxKt; 22 BxP, KtxP; 23 Kt–Kt4, KtxQBP! (proof of the depth of Bronstein's play on his 18th move); 24 B–R6 ch, K–R1; 25 Q–Kt2, P–Kt5; 26 BxR, and Black has a good game for the loss of the exchange. After the text-move White does threaten to play P–QKt3, and if Black tries the apparently effective 20 . . . , Kt–Q5?; then Tal intended

21 PxKt, PxP; 22 Kt–Q5, BxKt; 23 PxB, P–Q6; 24 QxB, PxB; 25 B–K3! (not Kt–K6 ch, K–Kt1). PxR=Q; 26 BxQ, Q–B4; 27 Kt–K6 ch. Black no doubt also considered these lines and accordingly selected a better move.

20	. . .	Kt–QR4
21	Kt–B3	Q–B2
22	Kt–Q5	BxKt

Better than 22 . . . , KtxKt; 23 PxKt, BxQP; 24 KtxP, with the threats of Kt–Kt4 and Q–K3.

23	PxB	KR–K1!
24	QxP	QxQ
25	KtxQ	

Bronstein was already running short of time and though he had played for this very position, he still has a difficult decision to make in selecting a continuation. He set great store by his centralized knight after KtxP and also by the threat of Kt–Kt6. Immediately after the game Tal showed that Black could have created great complications here by 25 . . . , B–Q3; 26 B–R6 ch, KxB; 27 KtxP ch, K–Kt2; 28 RxR, RxR; 29 KtxB, R–K7; 30 R–R1, RxB; 31 RxKt, RxKtP; with good drawing chances. Bronstein, however, rejected 25 . . . , B–Q3; exactly because of the sacrifice 26 B–R6 ch.

| 25 | . . . | KtxP |
| 26 | R–R1 | Kt–Kt6 |

Although he saw the possibility, Bronstein rightly did not risk the interesting move 26 . . . , Kt–Kt5?! White comes out better after 27 PxKt, BxP; 28 R–K3, B–B4; 29 RxKt, BxR; 30 BxB.

| 27 | BxKt | PxB |
| 28 | B–R6 ch! | |

(See diagram on page 101)

| 28 | . . . | K–Kt1? |

He should have accepted the sacrifice, but in the critical position after 28 . . . , KxB; 29 KtxP ch, K–Kt2; 30 KtxR, RxKt; he was afraid of the line 31 R–R5!, R–Kt1; 32

least a good proof of the fact that Tal does not attack in the *va banque* style of the 18th century but in the controlled and functional manner of a modern romantic. He seems to expect a simple end-game to emerge from the complications and to anticipate that after passing the maelstrom of combinative play he will reach terra firma beyond.

SICILIAN DEFENCE

	TAL	POLUGAEVSKY
1	P–K4	P–QB4
2	Kt–KB3	P–Q3
3	P–Q4	PxP
4	KtxP	Kt–KB3
5	Kt–QB3	P–QR3
6	B–Kt5	QKt–Q2
7	B–QB4	Q–R4
8	Q–Q2	P–K3
9	o–o	

Preferring a less well beaten track than that after 9 o–o–o.

9 ...   B–K2

P–Kt4 is hardly to be recommended because of 10 B–Q5!, PxB; 11 Kt–B6, Q–Kt3; 12 PxP. A game Mnatzakanian–Zurahov in the U. S. S. R. Championship semi-finals continued 12 ..., Kt–K4; 13 QR–K1, B–Kt2; 14 B–K3, Q–B2; 15 P–B4, BxKt; 16 PxKt, PxP; 17 PxB, B–K2; 18 B–Kt5, P–Kt5; 19 Kt–Q5. (Even better was 19 BxKt, PxKt; 20 Q–Q7 ch.) Larsen also came to grief against Tal with the move at Portoroz

10 QR–Q1   Kt–B4

A necessary move in Black's defensive system. o–o would be a mistake because of 11 Kt–Q5!

11 KR–K1   B–Q2
12 P–QR3!

Announcing his intention to attack. The natural reply 12 ..., Kt(B3)xP; does not

---

R–K5, B–Q1; 33 R–R7 ch, Kt–B2; when Black has a difficult position. Tal, on the other hand, was concerned about the line 31 R–R7, K–B1; 32 R–Kt7, B–B3; 33 RxP, KtxP; 34 PxKt, BxP. Actually, as Bronstein later found, there was a third line open, namely 31 R–R7, K–R3!; 32 R–Kt7, B–B3; 33 RxP, KtxP. After the text-move Black's game becomes hopeless.

29	Kt–B6	R–QB1
30	QR–Q1!	RxKt
31	RxKt	

The game now plays itself.

31	...	P–B3
32	RxP	P–Kt4
33	RxP	K–B2
34	R–Kt7	R–K3
35	RxR	KxR
36	P–R4	R–KKt1
37	P–KB4	B–B4 ch
38	K–B1	PxRP
39	R–Kt5	R–QB1
40	P–B5 ch	K–Q3
41	P–QKt4	P–R6
42	RxB	P–R7
43	B–B4 ch	Resigns

GAME 43

Tal crushed Polugaevsky by a combination which was neither complex nor original. The game, if not a great one, is at work because of 13 KtxKt, QxQ; 14 BxQ, KtxKt; 15 RxKt, P-Q4; 16 BxQP, PxB; 17 R-K2, K-B1; 18 B-Kt4, BxB; 19 PxB, and Black has little prospects in the ending with his weak pawns, his bad bishop and his undeveloped rook.

| 12 | ... | Q-B2 |
| 13 | P-QKt4 | Kt-R5 |

No better would be 13..., Kt(B4)xP; 14 KtxKt, QxB; 15 BxKt, PxB; 16 Kt-B5!

| 14 | KtxKt | BxKt |

15 BxKP!

A well calculated sacrifice and one of more value than many similar ones. It aims, as so many of Tal's combinations, at fixing the king in the centre and so making co-ordination of the black pieces difficult.

15	...	PxB
16	KtxP	QxP
17	Q-Q4!	K-B2
18	R-QB1	Q-R7
19	P-K5!	

KtxP leads to a doubtful ending after 19..., KxKt; 20 R-B7, Q-K3; 21 BxKt ch, QxB; 22 RxB ch K-Kt3. Correctly he plays to open further lines.

| 19 | ... | PxP? |

Also to be considered was QxKt, for after 20 PxKt, BxP; 21 BxB, QxB; 22 Q-Q5 ch,

K-B1; 23 R-K6, Black's position, though not easy, offers chances if he can reach an end-game.

20   QxP

| 20 | ... | QxP ch |

A clever idea, but one which simplifies without equalizing. Equally futile was 20..., KR-K1; 21 BxKt, BxB; 22 R-B7 ch, K-Kt1; 23 RxP ch. Even after 20..., Q-Q4; White has the initiative.

21	KxQ	Kt-Kt5 ch
22	K-Kt1	KtxQ
23	RxKt	BxB
24	KtxB ch	K-Kt3

If K-B3; 25 R(B1)-B5.

25   Kt-K6

To try and mate by R-K6 ch would be a mistake because of 25..., KxKt; 26 R-B5 ch, K-B5; 27 K-B2, B-B3!

25	...	KR-K1
26	R-K3	QR-B1
27	R-B1	B-Kt4
28	R-Kt3 ch	K-R3
29	KtxP	R-B1

There was more chance of drawing by BxR; 30 KtxR, RxKt; 31 KxB, R-K4.

| 30 | R-K1 | R-KB3 |
| 31 | P-R3 | R-QB7 |

32	R–K4	R–QB5
33	R–K5	R–QB8 ch
34	K–R2	Resigns

GAME 44

Variations on a theme ... A relationship between music and chess is well known and long established. André Danican Philidor, conductor of the French royal orchestra in the 18th century, was the greatest chess-player of his age. Francis Erkel, who composed the Hungarian national anthem and various operas, was an excellent and devoted chess-player. In our own days, both Smyslov and Taimanov have maintained close links with the world of music.

A kind of music pervades Tal's next game against Nikitin. It has its theme, a variation of the Sicilian Defence, played many times before in different orchestrations. It has its variations, the previous game against Polugaevsky, one against Larsen at Portoroz and many others. Now, with Black against Nikitin, he plays the very variation he rendered so questionable when he had White. This might have seemed to make things easier for Nikitin, but Tal makes this most dangerous line a glorious success, filled with boldness and charm. No one can quarrel with the orchestration, while the queen sacrifice is delightful. Nikitin died a most beautiful death!

SICILIAN DEFENCE

	NIKITIN	TAL
1	P–K4	P–QB4
2	Kt–KB3	P–Q3
3	P–Q4	PxP
4	KtxP	Kt–KB3
5	Kt–QB3	P–QR3
6	B–Kt5	QKt–Q2
7	B–QB4	Q–R4
8	Q–Q2	P–K3
9	0–0	P–R3
10	B–R4	B–K2
11	QR–K1	

Nikitin is treading in Tal's footsteps. The game has followed Tal–Larsen at Portoroz except that Tal there played 11 QR–Q1.

| 11 | ... | Kt–K4 |

Polugaevsky attacked White's KP by Kt–B4.

12	B–QKt3	P–KKt4
13	B–Kt3	B–Q2
14	P–B4	PxP
15	BxP	Q–B2

Apart from the fact that the rook is on K1 instead of Q1, the game has followed Tal–Larsen right up to this point. Larsen now went in for the poor line 15 ..., Kt–R4?. Tal prepares an attack on the white king.

16	Kt–B3	0–0–0
17	K–R1	KR–Kt1
18	B–K3	

White also prepares to attack the enemy king. Speed and coolness are pre-requisites in such positions.

18	...	B–B3
19	Q–Q4	R–Kt3
20	R–K2	

He who hesitates is lost.

20	...	R(Q1)–Kt1
21	Q–R7	KtxP
22	B–Kt6	

The complications are becoming severe, and Tal only now reveals how severe!

	22 ...	Kt(K5)xKt!

A magnificent sacrifice, which reveals that Tal has not entered the complications at random. The move is as much a delight to the romantics as to the mathematicians.

23	BxQ	KtxR

The harmonious co-ordination of the black pieces is most notable.

24	B–Kt6	RxP
25	B–R4	

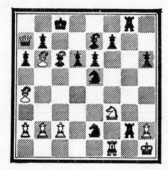

25 ...	R–Kt8 ch!

White is afloat in a sea of troubles. Tal prepares a winning ending out of a succession of combinations.

26	BxR	RxB ch

The proper and forceful method of continuing was 26 ..., BxKt ch; 27 RxB, RxB ch; 28 QxR, KtxQ; for though Tal reaches the identical position, White could have put a spoke in his wheel by 27 RxR, though even then Black has a material advantage.

27	QxR	BxKt ch
28	RxB	KtxQ
29	R–B3 ch	K–Q1

30	KxKt	P–Q4
31	R–KKt3	

Tal had to see as far ahead as this point. Now his passed pawns decide the issue and it is merely a question of technique.

31 ...	B–Kt4

Limiting the action of the white rook.

32	P–Kt4	P–Kt4
33	B–Kt3	P–B4
34	P–B3	K–K2
35	P–QR4	P–B5
36	R–R3	Kt–B5
37	PxP	PxP
38	K–B2	K–Q3
39	K–K2	P–K4
40	BxKt	KtPxB
41	R–R5	P–K5
42	P–R4	P–B6 ch
43	K–Q1	B–B5
	Resigns	

Having thought it over during the adjournment, White did not resume.

GAME 45

Tal finds the Benoni Defence peculiarly suited to his style and handles it energetically in the following game against Geller. The position is full of tension at a very early stage and one small error gives Tal the advantage. His method of asserting this advantage is, however, worthy of study in the way he forestalls every counter-move.

BENONI DEFENCE

	GELLER	TAL
1	P–Q4	Kt–KB3
2	P–QB4	P–B4
3	P–Q5	P–K3
4	Kt–QB3	PxP
5	PxP	P–Q3
6	P–K4	P–KKt3
7	Kt–B3	

Avoiding the hazards of the sharper P–B4.

7	...	B–Kt2
8	B–Kt5	P–QR3
9	P–QR4	P–R3
10	B–KB4	B–Kt5
11	B–K2	O–O
12	O–O	R–K1
13	Q–B2	Q–B2

A move that occurs in many variations of the Benoni Defence. It has the advantages of preventing White's P–K5 and of giving the queen an active role.

14	KR–K1	QKt–Q2
15	P–R3	

Kt–Q2 would have served White's purpose better. Black's counter-play develops quickly now.

15	...	BxKt
16	BxB	P–B5!

An energetic advance which has as its aim White's KP.

17	B–K2	QR–B1
18	P–R5	Kt–B4!

Tal's plan materializes with all his pieces taking a useful part. White cannot defend the KP even by 19 P–B3, because afterwards he would be driven back by 19 ..., Kt–Kt6. His only reply is the move chosen.

19	BxBP	Kt(B3)xKP
20	KtxKt	RxKt
21	RxR	KtxR
22	QxKt	QxB
23	Q–B3?	

An error so slight as scarcely to be an error. But if 23 QxQ, RxQ; 24 BxQP, R–Q5!; Tal reaches an end-game where the issue is decided by the merest nuance of a tempo. Relatively best was 23 R–R4, Q–B7; 24 QxQ, RxQ; 25 BxQP, R–Q7; 26 R–QKt4, RxQP; 27 B–B7, R–QKt4; and a draw is almost certain.

23	...	Q–Kt5
24	Q–KKt3	QxKtP
25	R–K1	

He has little choice but to play for a K-side attack.

25	...	Q–Kt4
26	Q–KB3	B–B1
27	P–R4	QxRP
28	R–Kt1	P–QKt4
29	P–R5	P–Kt4
30	Q–KKt3	Q–R7
31	R–Q1	Q–K7
32	R–Q3	B–Kt2!

Tal's play is an object-lesson. He gives up the QP, which had no great value anyway, and turns to a counter-attack which virtually eliminates White's aggression.

33	Q–R3	

White has to change his plan. R–Q2 would be answered by 33 ..., Q–K8ch; after which Black can quietly steal the bishop.

33	. . .	R–B7
34	BxQP	R–B8 ch
35	K–R2	QxP

The game is lost for White. Tal now simplifies by means of mating threats.

36	R–KB3	Q–Kt8 ch
37	K–Kt3	Q–K8 ch

38	K–R2	B–K4 ch
39	BxB	QxB ch
40	Q–Kt3	QxP
41	R–Q3	Q–QB4
42	Q–Kt4	Q–K4 ch
	Resigns	

For after 43 P–Kt3, B–B7 ch; 44 K–R3, Q–K3; Black has a winning ending.

Just as at Munich the year before, Tal turned out to be the unexpected success of the tournament. The Swiss organizers had originally asked Botvinnik to compete in this their Jubilee tournament. The World Champion, in declining the invitation, turned to Tal who was standing beside him, placed his hand on Tal's shoulder and said: "Invite the future world champion instead!" It was a good recommendation, for Tal won first prize.

This win was indeed a strong hint as to who would be the next champion. To come out ahead of Keres, Gligoric, and Bobby Fischer was almost as great a success as his win at Portoroz, especially when it is borne in mind that lower down the table were such players as Barcza, Unzicker and Larsen. Tal was now indeed a candidate for world honours.

GAME 46

Tal was beaten in the first round of the 150th Anniversary tournament of the Zurich Schachgesellschaft and the following game, played in the second round, introduced a series of nine successive wins. It is a typical short game packed with combinations. Tal's clock showed little more than an hour for such a game!

SICILIAN DEFENCE

	KUPPER	TAL
1	P–K4	P–QB4
2	Kt–KB3	P–Q3
3	P–Q4	PxP
4	KtxP	Kt–KB3
5	Kt–QB3	P–QR3
6	B–Kt5	P–K3
7	P–B4	P–Kt4

An unusual move, the normal lines being Q–Kt3 or P–R3 or B–K2.

| 8 | Q–B3 |

Gligoric's 8 P–K5!, is certainly more energetic.

8	...	B–Kt2
9	B–Q3	B–K2
10	O–O–O	Q–Kt3!
11	KR–K1	QKt–Q2
12	Kt(B3)–K2	

Kupper is already at a disadvantage. But the bolder 12 Kt–Q5!?, only forces Black to win two knights for a rook by 12 .... QxKt; 13 Kt–B7 ch, K–Q1; 14 KtxR, Q–B4!; because 12 ..., PxKt; is met by 13 Kt–B5!

| 12 | ... | Kt–B4 |
| 13 | BxKt? | |

Kt–KKt3 would have infused some life into White's game. Now Tal is able to attack strongly.

| 13 | ... | BxB |
| 14 | P–KKt4 | |

14 ...   Kt–R5!

Inducing a weakening of the king's position.

15   P–B3

His hopes of playing 15 P–Kt5, have to be postponed because of 15..., BxKt; 16 KtxB, KtxP; 17 BxP ch, PxB; 18 KxKt, o–o: and Black has the superior position.

15   ...   P–Kt5
16   B–B2

16   ...   KtxKtP!

The threat bears fruit. Tal's sacrifice displays speed and beauty.

17   KxKt   PxP dbl. ch
18   KxP   o–o
19   R–QKt1

B–Kt3 would be answered by the advance of the QRP.

19   ...   Q–R4 ch!
20   K–Q3   QR–B1
21   Q–B2   B–R1

There is even time for this quiet move!

22   R–Kt3   P–K4
23   P–Kt5

23   ...   PxKt

Adding another little complication, for now Kupper has to worry about the loose position of his bishop.

24   KtxP

If 24 PxB, there is a spectacular win by 24..., RxB!; 25 KxR, QxP ch; 26 R–Kt2, BxP ch!

24   ...   BxKt
      Resigns

GAME 47

The young Danish grandmaster, Larsen, has often won by means of his deep defensive play. The following positional struggle might therefore be reckoned to favour him psychologically, but Tal proves himself equally at home in this field.

SICILIAN DEFENCE

	TAL	LARSEN
1	P–K4	P–QB4
2	Kt–KB3	Kt–QB3
3	P–Q4	PxP
4	KtxP	P–KKt3
5	Kt–QB3	

Omitting the usual 5 P–QB4, leading into the Simagin variation.

5	...	B–Kt2
6	B–K3	Kt–B3
7	B–QB4	o–o
8	B–Kt3	P–Q3
9	P–B3	KtxKt

Larsen may have been considering the 9 ..., B–K3!? line, but he avoids complications against so renowned a tactician as Tal.

10	BxKt	B–K3
11	Q–Q2	Q–R4
12	o–o–o	P–QKt4
13	K–Kt1	P–Kt5

14 Kt–Q5!

The game moves onto positional lines; an exchange on Q5 is now forced and the strength or weakness of the pawn position will decide the issue.

14	...	BxKt
15	PxB	Q–Kt4

16	KR–K1	P–QR4
17	Q–K2	

He is quite pleased to force the exchange of queens, as his advantage in space is then more readily exploited.

17	...	QxQ
18	RxQ	P–R5
19	B–B4	KR–B1
20	B–Kt5	R–R4
21	BxKt	

Prudently avoiding 21 B–B6?, KtxP!

21	...	BxB
22	B–B6	P–R6
23	P–QKt3	K–B1

24 P–QB4!

Mobilizing the Q side in readiness for action by the pieces. Even if Black avoids exchange of pawns, 25 R–K4, will be strong. Nevertheless, the strength of the move is above all psychological, for Black is actually deluded into dreaming of a win. With 24 ..., P–K4; followed by B–Q1–Kt3 and R–R2 White would be checked. Black, however, misjudges the dynamic strength of White's QKtP in thinking that with a pawn ahead and bishops of opposite colours he cannot well go wrong. But go wrong he does on the 25th move and even more so on the 26th.

24	...	PxP e. p.
25	K–B2	R–R2?
26	P–QKt4	P–K3?

Black's position collapses. Better was P–K4 followed by B–Q1.

27	P–Kt5	PxP
28	P–Kt6!	R–K2
29	RxR	KxR
30	R–K1 ch	

Winning a piece by the threat of 31 R–K8 ch.

30	...	B–K4
31	P–Kt7	R–QKt1
32	P–B4	K–K3
33	PxB	PxP
34	R–QKt1	K–Q3
35	R–Kt6	P–Q5
36	R–R6	P–B4
37	R–R8	K–B2
38	B–Q5	P–K5
39	RxP	P–K6
40	K–Q3	P–Kt4
41	KxP!	Resigns

For now the pawns begin to fall.

GAME 48

One of the myths of the ancient Greeks tells how Amphion, the poet, raised the walls of Thebes entirely by the music of his lyre. One cannot but recall this story when looking at Tal's game with Unzicker, when out of nothing he creates a combination as if by magic. His pawn sacrifice is wholly admirable.

SICILIAN DEFENCE

UNZICKER   TAL

1	P–K4	P–QB4
2	Kt–KB3	P–K3
3	P–Q4	PxP
4	KtxP	P–QR3

5	P–QB4	Kt–KB3
6	Kt–QB3	B–Kt5
7	B–Q2	

The variation beginning with 7 B–Q3, has proved better in practice, though Black gets counter-play by 7 . . . , Kt–B3; 8 Kt–B2, BxKt ch; 9 PxB, P–Q4!; 10 KPxP, PxP, 11 0–0, B–K3.

7	...	0–0
8	P–K5	BxKt!

More energetic than 8 . . . , Kt–K1; 9 Kt–B2; B–K2; 10 B–Q3, with an attack.

9	BxB	Kt–K5
10	Q–B2	P–Q4
11	PxP e. p.	KtxB!

A splendid interpolation. After 11 . . . , KtxQP; 12 0–0–0, White gets a strong attack. Tal's line allows Black to gain the initiative.

12	QxKt	QxP
13	R–Q1	

Routine moves are little help against Tal. He should have completed his development with 13 B–K2.

13	...	P–K4!

A surprising pawn sacrifice, which proves of full value. Tal is now on the attack.

14 Kt-B3	Q-KKt3
15 B-Q3	

He cannot take the pawn. If 15 QxP, B-Kt5!; 16 B-K2, Kt-B3; 17 Q-B3, KR-K1; with a strong attack. Or 15 KtxP, R-K1; 16 B-K2, QxP; 17 K-Q2, Q-Kt4 ch; winning a piece.

15 ...	P-K5!

His bold 13th move now gains in stature! Black's central superiority proves vital in this interesting position.

16 B-Kt1	P-B4!
17 Kt-R4	Q-K3
18 P-KKt3	Kt-B3
19 R-Q5	

Finding the best continuation, though he cannot avoid the loss of a pawn.

19 ...	Q-B2
20 O-O	B-K3
21 R-Q6	

21 ...	BxP

After eight moves Tal's pawn sacrifice has led to the win of a pawn. He now makes a few energetic defensive moves to parry White's threats.

22 R(B1)-Q1	B-K3
23 B-B2	QR-K1
24 Kt-Kt2	Q-B3!
25 QxQ	

25 Q-B5!, offered more chances, but Tal still had the edge after 25..., Q-K2. For example, I. 26 Q-Kt6, B-B1; 27 B-R4, R-Q1. II. 26 Kt-B4, B-B1; 27 Kt-Q5, Q-K4. III. 26 B-R4!, BxP; 27 P-Kt3, R-Q1; 28 Q-B4 ch, K-R1; 29 RxR, RxR; 30 RxR ch, KtxR; 31 Q-B2, P-QKt4; 32 QxB, Q-Kt5!

25 ...	RxQ
26 P-QR3	Kt-K4
27 Kt-B4	B-B2
28 RxR	PxR
29 R-Q6	

29 K-Kt2, would have been a little better, as the black rook is later able to infiltrate into White's position.

29 ...	Kt-B6 ch
30 K-R1	R-QB1
31 B-Q1	R-B8
32 R-Q8 ch	K-Kt2
33 K-Kt2	

Against 33..., B-Kt6.

33 ...	Kt-K8 ch
34 K-R3	

34 ...	Kt-Q6!

An amusing little move which wins more pawns by closing the file.

35 B-K2	KtxKt ch
36 PxKt	R-B7
Resigns	

GAME 49

One would have to go far to find a more characteristic Tal game than that against Nievergelt, which displays in the highest degree his militant point of view and his ever-present will to win. His own analysis in the Zurich Tournament book reflects his views as though they were an absolute creed, and we shall have the pleasure of quoting his analysis at two points later on.

SICILIAN DEFENCE

	TAL	NIEVERGELT
1	P–K4	P–QB4
2	Kt–KB3	Kt–QB3
3	P–Q4	PxP
4	KtxP	Kt–B3
5	Kt–QB3	P–Q3
6	B–KKt5	P–K3
7	Q–Q2	P–KR3

There was no hurry for this. P–QR3 is necessary.

| 8 | BxKt | PxB |

Forced, since 8..., QxB; would be answered by 9 Kt(Q4)–Kt5, a line which 7..., P–QR3; would have forestalled, thus preserving his pawn skeleton, which is now disrupted.

9	0–0–0	P–R3
10	P–B4	B–Q2
11	B–K2!	

A strong move, which proved its value in the Bondarevsky–Botvinnik game in the XIXth Championship, where Botvinnik did not answer, as Nievergelt here, with 11.... P–KR4; but tried 11..., Q–Kt3. After 12 B–R5!, KtxKt; 13 QxKt, QxQ; 14 RxQ, R–KKt1; 15 P–KKt3, Black had the worst of it.

| 11 | ... | P–KR4 |
| 12 | K–Kt1 | Q–Kt3 |

| 13 | Kt–Kt3 | 0–0–0 |
| 14 | KR–B1 | |

Identical so far with the Keres–Botvinnik game at the Alekhine Memorial tournament in Moscow in 1956. Keres got much the better position after 14..., Kt–R4; 15 R–B3, KtxKt; 16 RPxKt, K–Kt1; 17 Kt–R4, Q–R2; 18 P–B5. Nievergelt tries to improve on this line.

14	...	B–K2
15	R–B3	QR–Kt1
16	B–B1	K–Kt1
17	R–Q3!	

It is most noticeable how often Tal manages to get his rooks into action in quite an early stage of the game.

17	...	B–QB1
18	P–QR3	P–R5
19	Q–K1	R–Kt5

The following knight sacrifice could have been avoided by 19..., B–B1. Unlike the majority of commentators, who therefore recommend that move for Black, Tal agrees with Nievergelt's choice as permitting a more active defence. With this view we must agree, since 19..., B–B1; would have allowed White to build up an attack fairly rapidly by regrouping his pieces.

| 20 | Kt–Q5 | PxKt |
| 21 | PxP | Kt–K4 |

22	PxKt	BPxP
23	Kt–R5	B–Q1

Only envisaging the withdrawal of the knight, but the outcome is very different!

| 24 | Kt–B6 ch! | |

An unpleasant surprise for Black. It is not the actual offer of the knight that is original–after all, its capture would cost the queen–but the various plans which Tal has conceived as arising out of the move.

24	...	K–R1
25	R–QKt3	Q–B2

| 26 | R–QB3?! | |

Tal made this move instantaneously, and he too queries it. This is his explanation: "After 26 KtxB, QxKt; there is no trace of an attack left and Black has the better position. Therefore I decided on the piece sacrifice. I am well aware I was criticized for it–it wasn't correct, I was just lucky, I spoofed my opponent, my game was hopelessly lost and so on. Well, I couldn't see where I was so hopelessly lost, and in any case why worry about the critics? I have the satisfaction of knowing that the followers of chess, the spectators and the readers, are delighted when grandmasters take chances and are not merely woodshifting."

26	...	PxKt
27	RxP	Q–Kt2!

Best, according to Tal, since in reply to 28 BxP, he could then sacrifice his queen with more than sufficient material compensation.

28	RxP	R–R5
29	R–Q3	B–B2

The best defence was P–K5, after which Black had good drawing chances.

30	R–KB6	B–Q1
31	R–B6	P–K5

Too late now. Since the white rook is now on QB6, Q–B3 will gain a tempo.

| 32 | R–QKt3 | B–R4 |

Forced by the threat of Q–B3, which would attack two pieces.

33	Q–K3	Q–R2
34	Q–R6!	

Deciding the issue. Of this move Tal wrote: "A tremendous surprise! The intervention of the queen is decisive and there is no defence. Without taking chances earlier, such a position could scarcely have been reached. Lasker and Alekhine taught us that chess is a fight!"

34	...	R–Q1
35	BxP	B–Q7
36	Q–B6	Q–Q2
37	BxB	Resigns

GAME 50

The game against Keller is rich in combinations, and though they may have flaws, the whole attack is so rich in ideas that it is easy to overlook them. Pushkin once said that when Russian was spoken in dialect or with small grammatical errors, it only became more charming; lacking the affectation of perfection, it came nearer to life. And so it is with this game.

SLAV DEFENCE

	TAL	KELLER
1	Kt–KB3	Kt–KB3
2	P–B4	P–K3
3	Kt–B3	P–Q4
4	P–Q4	P–B3
5	B–Kt5	PxP
6	P–K4	P–Kt4
7	P–QR4	

More common is 7 P–K5, leading to equally sharp play after 7..., P–KR3; 8 B–R4, P–Kt4; 9 KKtxP, PxKt; 10 BxKtP, QKt–Q2; 11 PxKt, Q–Kt3.

| 7 | ... | Q–Kt3 |

The correct move. After 7..., P–Kt5; 8 Kt–QKt1, P–KR3; 9 BxKt, QxB; 10 BxP, Q–Kt3; 11 QKt–Q2, QxKtP; 12 R–KKt1, Q–R6; 13 Q–Kt3, and 14 o–o–o!, White has a strong game.

8	BxKt	PxB
9	B–K2	P–QR3
10	o–o	B–QKt2
11	P–Q5!	BPxP
12	KPxP	P–Kt5

Keller is already at a disadvantage, psychologically at least, for he is threatened with an exchange on his QKt4, followed by P–QKt3 by White, and his Q-side pawn skeleton ceases to exist. So he is virtually forced to play the text-move.

| 13 | P–R5 | Q–B2 |
| 14 | PxP?! | |

Kt–QR4 would have been sufficient to demonstrate an advantage for White, but Tal is always happy to fish in muddy waters. The very rarity of such decisions enriches the literature of the game. The move is justified, moreover, in the light of subsequent analysis.

14	...	PxKt
15	Kt–Q4	R–Kt1
16	Q–R4 ch	K–Q1

Obviously if 16..., B–B3; 17 PxP ch, KxP; 18 QxP ch.

17	P–KKt3	B–Q4
18	KR–Q1	K–B1
19	KtPxP	B–B4

| 20 | P–K7! | |

Stepping up his attack. The pawn causes Keller a lot of trouble.

| 20 | ... | Kt–B3? |

BxP was necessary, though Tal still had an attack after 21 Kt–B5, B–K3; 22 KtxB ch, QxKt; 23 BxP.

| 21 | B–Kt4 ch! | K–Kt2 |

| 22 | Kt–Kt5! | |

Attacking the queen but with an eye chiefly to the king. The knight cannot be captured because 23 QxP ch, would utterly destroy Black's position.

22	...	Q–K4
23	R–K1	B–K5

There is nothing better, for Q–Kt4 would be answered by 24 QR–Q1.

24   QR–Kt1!

A witty combination! If 24..., BxR; 25 RxB. Meanwhile, White is threatening 25 RxB!, QxR; 26 Kt–Q6 dbl. ch, which Keller plays to prevent.

24	...	RxB
25	RxB!	

Still it comes!

| 25 | ... | QxR |

Forced, for after RxR a staggering display of pin and counter-pin follows, as for example 26 Kt–Q4 dis. ch, Kt–Kt5; 27 Q–B6 ch, K–Kt1 (K–R2; 28 Q–Q7 ch, K–Kt1; 29 Kt–B6 mate); 28 Q–K8 ch, K–Kt2; 29 Q–Q7 ch, Q–B2; 30 Q–Q5 ch, winning a rook and the game.

26   Kt–Q6 dbl. ch!

Winning the queen, but it is still far from easy to win the game.

26	...	K–B2
27	KtxQ	RxKt
28	Q–Q1	R–K4

RxP would have made it even more difficult for White.

29   R–Kt7 ch!

Yet another combination!

29	...	KxR
30	Q–Q7 ch	K–Kt1
31	P–K8=Q ch	RxQ
32	QxR ch	K–Kt2
33	Q–Q7 ch	K–Kt1
34	QxKt	Resigns

GAME 51

Walther allowed Tal to obtain the initiative right in the opening. Retribution was immediate and led to another Tal effort which ended with a nice point on the 30th move.

SICILIAN DEFENCE

WALTHER   TAL

1	P–K4	P–QB4
2	Kt–KB3	P–K3
3	Kt–B3	P–QR3
4	P–Q4	PxP
5	KtxP	Q–B2
6	B–Q3	Kt–QB3!

Tal has already equalized without effort.

7   KtxKt?

B–K3 was better. The text-move merely strengthens Black's centre, as White cannot contest it with P–QB4.

7	...	KtPxKt
8	o–o	Kt–B3
9	P–B4	P–Q4
10	Q–B3	B–Kt2
11	B–Q2	

An artificial move, instead of the more accurate R–K1, which would make 11 ..., P–B4; more difficult.

11   ...   P–B4!

He already has the initiative, and that is dangerous enough with Tal behind it!

12   PxP

12	...	P–B5!
13	B–K4	PxP
14	B–B5	

Of course not 14 BxP, Q–B4 ch.

14	...	B–B4 ch
15	K–R1	P–Kt3
16	QR–K1 ch	K–B1
17	Kt–R4	P–Q5!

Tal prefers to offer a sacrifice rather than accept one! In fact, 17 ..., PxB; would be bad on account of 18 KtxB, QxKt; 19 B–B3!, Q–Kt3 (Q–Q3; 20 B–K5!); 20 Q–R3, P–Q5; 21 Q–R6 ch, K–Kt1; 22 R–K3!

18	Q–KR3	K–Kt2
19	KtxB	QxKt
20	R–K5	Q–B3
21	R–B3	KR–K1
22	R–KKt3	

22   ...   P–B6!

The opening of lines is catastrophic for White.

23	PxP	PxP
24	RxP	

BxP is answered by Q–B5!

24	...	Q–Kt3
25	B–K3	

He had to try and prevent 25 ..., Q–B7.

25	...	Q–Kt8 ch
26	B–Kt1	

| 26 | ... | B–K5! |

A fine move, in Tal's most harmonious style.

| 27 | BxB |

Forced. 27 B–Kt4, is answered by Kt–Q4!

27	...	KtxB
28	R–B3	QR–Q1
29	P–Kt3	RxR
30	PxR	

| 30 | ... | Q–Kt2! |

Most effective, for if now 31 Q–Kt2, then 31 ..., R–Q7!; 32 R–Kt3, KtxP ch!

Resigns

GAME 52

The Benoni Defence arouses mixed opinions and many experts are sceptical of its value. Many of Tal's games, and not least the following against Donner, show him to be a strong supporter of the defence. His modern methods of treating it are exciting and it is notable how he foils White's attempts to break through in the centre while he himself succeeds in breaking through on the Q side.

BENONI DEFENCE

	DONNER	TAL
1	P–Q4	Kt–KB3
2	P–QB4	P–B4
3	P–Q5	P–K3
4	Kt–QB3	PxP
5	PxP	P–Q3
6	Kt–B3	

The sharper continuation is 6 P–K4.

6	...	P–KKt3
7	P–K4	B–Kt2
8	B–Q3?	

An error already, the importance of which is highlighted by Tal's energetic play. 8 B–K2, followed by 9 B–Kt5, was reasonable enough.

8	...	O–O
9	O–O	

If he tries to forestall the pin of the knight by 9 P–KR3, Black replies 9 ..., P–QKt4!

9	...	P–QR3
10	P–QR4	B–Kt5!
11	P–R3	BxKt
12	QxB	QKt–Q2

Black's position is flexible, to say the least. His advance on the Q side cannot be prevented, while White's central advance is hindered by his control of his K4. In such positions the traditional advantages, such as possession of two bishops, have only an imaginary importance. In the following play Tal's advantage is increased with every move.

13	B–KB4	Q–B2
14	Q–K2	KR–K1
15	B–R2?	

With the wholly faulty plan of advancing the KP, which he can never realise owing to Tal's activity on the queen's wing. Better was 15 KR–B1, to check Black's counterplay.

15	...	QR–B1
16	B–QB4	Kt–K4!

This regrouping brings Tal's pieces into their customary faultless co-ordination. White is loth to exchange by 17 BxKt, because he wishes to retain the bishop to assist the central advance.

17	P–B4	KtxB
18	QxKt	Kt–Q2
19	KR–K1	

Still pinning his hopes on a break-through, but now Tal produces a fine idea for starting his counter-play.

19	...	Q–Kt3!

Attaining the strategical aim of the Benoni Defence, infiltration on the Q side. Q–Kt5 cannot now be prevented.

20	QR–Kt1	Q–Kt5
21	Q–B1	

An admission of failure. Nor would exchange of queens have helped, as Black would then have overrun the Q side and broken through there. Even now his pawns gain predominance.

21	...	P–B5!
22	R–K2	P–QKt4
23	PxP	PxP
24	K–R1	BxKt

The very mainspring of the Benoni Defence, the proud bishop on KKt2, is exchanged, for now the passed QBP must win.

25	PxB	QxP
26	RxP	Q–Q6!

It is quite astonishing how rapidly Donner's position collapses.

27	Q–K1	P–B6
28	R–Kt1	Kt–B4!
	Resigns	

For after 29 P–K5, P–B7, 30 R–B1, Kt–Kt6; Black wins easily.

THE CANDIDATES' TOURNAMENT, YUGOSLAVIA, 1959

There were marked similarities between the AVRO tournament of 1938 in Holland and the Yugoslav Candidates' Tournament twenty-one years later. Both these wandering chess circuses, which moved from city to city, were marathon contests of outstanding quality. Moreover, the hero of both tournaments was the grandmaster Paul Keres; first in the AVRO tournament, he was the first favourite also in the Candidates' tournament, and indeed his play justified this for in the end he only fell below Mikhail Tal. As for Tal, now winner of a Candidates' tournament, this was indeed the fulfilment of a dream; he had but one more hurdle on the way to the world title, a match with Botvinnik, and now that too was assured.

Tal played with immense energy throughout the tournament, setting such a pace that even Keres was left a full point and a half behind. Alekhine and Lasker used at times to play for victory in a similar frenzy of dedication. One can perhaps best form an opinion of Tal by reading the statement he made at the end of the tournament: "My play was uneven, though in so long a tournament it is difficult to maintain a constant standard throughout. In the first series I was rather feeling my way because I was in poor physical shape, and I was really only at my best during the third series in Zagreb. My best games, I think, were those against Smyslov in the second series and Fischer in the third. But the real hero of the tournament was Paul Keres, for in spite of his 43 years he fought with all the vigour of a young man in his twenties . . ."

GAME 53

One of Tal's outstanding games! His play is original right from the outset, the opening being handled in close fashion at first but then opened up on the 5th move. With Smyslov failing to find the best defence, Tal secures a dangerous initiative against the black king and after Smyslov's counterattack he winds up with a fine queen sacrifice.

CARO-KANN DEFENCE

	TAL	SMYSLOV
1	P–K4	P–QB3
2	P–Q3	P–Q4

3	Kt–Q2	P–K4
4	KKt–B3	Kt–Q2
5	P–Q4!	

A surprise after what has gone before.

5	. . .	PxKP
6	QKtxP	PxP
7	QxP	KKt–B3
8	B–KKt5	B–K2
9	0–0–0	0–0
10	Kt–Q6	Q–R4
11	B–QB4	P–Kt4

Hoping to show that White's last move was too energetic, for now if 12 B–Kt3?, P–B4 and 13 . . . , P–B5; will win the piece. Tal,

however, finds an answer which not only
saves the bishop but allows the queen to
take up a strong post in front of the black
king.

| 12 | B–Q2! | Q–R3 |

Possibly with the idea of switching the
queen along the third rank later so as to
defend the king, but he never gets time for
this. An alternative, leading to great complications, was 12 . . . , Q–R5; 13 Kt–B5,
B–B4; 14 Q–R4!; QxB; 15 Q–Kt5, Kt–K1;
16 KR–K1!, P–B3; 17 Q–Kt3, QxP; 18 B–B3,
P–Kt3; 19 Kt–Kt5!, though Black can avoid
this line with 13 . . . , B–Q1; when White's
best move is probably the simple 14 B–Kt3.
The text-move wins a piece but with considerable risk.

| 13 | Kt–B5 | B–Q1! |

Although after 13 . . . , B–B4?; 14 Q–R4,
PxB; 15 KtxP?, Black wins by BxP; 16 QxB,
QxP; 17 B–B3, Kt–K5; White can refute
the line by 15 B–B3, QxP; 16 RxKt!, BxR;
17 Kt–R6 ch, K–R1; 18 QxKt!, with an
elegant mate.

| 14 | Q–R4 | PxB |

He must take the risk now, for if 14 . . . ,
Kt–Q4; 15 Q–Kt3, B–B3; 16 BxKt, followed
by 17 K–Kt1, gives White an advantageous
position.

15	Q–Kt5	Kt–R4
16	Kt–R6 ch	K–R1
17	QxKt	QxP

The decisive mistake. Probably best was
17 . . . , B–B3; 18 KtxP ch, K–Kt1; 19
Kt(B3)–Kt5, BxKt; 20 KtxB, Kt–B3; 21
Q–R4 QxP; 22 B–B3 B–B4; with fairly
good chances. Also worth considering was
17 . . . , PxKt, 18 QxRP, P–B3; 19 Kt–Kt5
PxKt; 20 B–B3 ch, B–B3; 21 RxKt, BxR;
22 BxB ch, RxB; 23 QxR ch, K–Kt1; with
a probable draw.

| 18 | B–B3 | Kt–B3 |

If 18 . . . , B–B3; 19 KtxP ch, K–Kt1; 20
Kt(B3)–Kt5, P–KR3; 21 KtxP ch!, leads to
mate, while if 18 . . . , P–B3; 19 KR–K1!, is
extremely strong. White now exploits the
weakness of the back rank with a fine queen
sacrifice.

| 19 | QxP! | Q–R8 ch |
| 20 | K–Q2 | RxQ |

Or 20 . . . , QxR ch; 21 RxQ, RxQ; 22
KtxR ch, K–Kt1; 23 KtxB, winning a
piece.

21	KtxR ch	K–Kt1
22	RxQ	KxKt
23	Kt–K5 ch	K–K3
24	KtxP(B6)	Kt–K5 ch
25	K–K3	B–Kt3 ch
26	B–Q4	Resigns

GAME 54

Fischer, the young American prodigy who is the junior of all grandmasters, plays his favourite 6 B–QB4, variation against Tal's Sicilian Defence. Tal responds in unorthodox fashion by postponing the development of his QKt, and because Fischer fails to recognize the importance of this, he finds himself in difficulties as early as the 11th move. By the 17th move Black has established a winning game and the victory is obtained by a combination of positional and combinative motifs which is almost faultless.

SICILIAN DEFENCE

	FISCHER	TAL
1	P–K4	P–QB4
2	Kt–KB3	P–Q3
3	P–Q4	PxP
4	KtxP	Kt–KB3
5	Kt–QB3	P–QR3
6	B–QB4	P–K3
7	B–Kt3	

Olafsson, in the same tournament, tried 7 P–QR3, against Fischer, with the idea of retreating the bishop to QR2 and so avoiding its later exchange. The games of this tournament went a long way to shedding light on this particular opening complex.

| 7 | . . . | B–K2 |

In a later game with Fischer from the 27th round, the score of which follows later, Tal tried the wilder P–QKt4 and got into difficulties. The key factor is the delay in developing the QKt, the importance of which appears on the 10th and 11th moves.

8	P–B4	0–0
9	Q–B3	Q–B2
10	0–0	

The value of holding up development of the QKt is now apparent. If 10 P–B5,

Kt–B3; exchanging off the white knight and so protecting K3.

| 10 | . . . | P–QKt4 |
| 11 | P–B5? | |

It was vital to play P–QR3 so as to impede Black's next move.

| 11 | . . . | P–Kt5 |

Now it can be equally seen why Black has not developed his knight via Q2, since he now still has his K3 defended. If now 12 PxP (which would be strong if the Kt were on Q2), PxKt; 13 PxP ch, K–R1; 14 PxP, B–Kt5; and White has insufficient compensation for his piece.

| 12 | Kt–R4 |

Of course not 12 Kt(B3)–K2, P–K4; winning a piece. Even 12 Kt–Q1, is disadvantageous after 12 . . ., P–K4; 13 Kt–K2, B–Kt2; 14 Kt–Kt3, Kt–B3! An attempt to complicate by 12 P–K5, would not help because of 12 . . ., PxKt!; 13 QxR, QPxP; 14 Kt–K2, B–B4 ch; 15 K–R1, B–Kt2!

12	. . .	P–K4
13	Kt–K2	B–Kt2
14	Kt–Kt3	QKt–Q2

At last it is time to develop the knight!

| 15 | B–K3 |

After 15 B–Q2, P–QR4; 16 P–B3, B–B3!; he cannot play 17 PxP, without losing a piece, while 17 QR–B1, would be met by 17 . . ., Q–Kt2; and 18 . . ., P–Q4. The best line was probably 15 P–B4, B–B3; 16 Q–K2, KR–B1; 17 B–Kt5, BxKt; 18 BxB, Kt–Kt3; 19 B–Kt3, KtxBP; and White has good chances in spite of the loss of a pawn.

| 15 | . . . | B–B3 |
| 16 | B–B2 | Q–Kt2 |

16 . . ., Q–R4?; so far from winning a piece, would actually turn out disadvantageous to Black after 17 P–QR3!

17   ...   P–Q4!

A central break-through of this kind is normally decisive. Black has strong pressure in the centre and along the long diagonal and that is enough to put Tal in his element.

18	PxP	KtxP
19	Kt–K4	

An attempt to keep his grip on part of the centre. If 19 BxKt, BxB; 20 Kt–K4, Black gets a considerable advantage by 20 ..., QR–B1.

19   ...   Kt–B5!

Threatening Kt–B3 with a quick decision.

20   P–B4

So as to defend the knight by B–B2, but P–B3 leaving the bishop's present diagonal open was preferable. 20 P–Kt3?, is no good against 20 ..., Kt–R6 ch; 21 K–Kt2, Kt–Kt4. Tal now gives the game a surprising twist which would not have been possible after 20 P–B3.

20   ...   P–Kt3!

An innocent looking little move which triggers off an exceptionally strong K-side attack.

21   PxP

White's position is hardly enviable after 21 P–Kt4, PxP; 22 PxP, K–R1.

21	...	P–B4!
22	P–Kt7	

The only way to avoid loss of a piece

22	...	KxP
23	Q–Kt3 ch	K–R1
24	Kt(K4)–B5	

Otherwise 24 ..., R–KKt1; wins at once.

24	...	KtxKt
25	BxKt	BxB ch
26	KtxB	Q–QB2

Avoiding the error 26 ..., Q–K2; 27 QxKt.

27	Q–K3	QR–K1
28	R–K2	

He has nothing better. If 28 P–Kt3, either Kt–Kt7; or stronger still Kt–R6 ch; 29 K–B1, P–B5!

28	...	KtxR ch
29	QxKt	BxP
30	KtxP	Q–R2 ch
31	KxB	

If 31 P-B5, B-Kt2; 32 B-B4, BxKt; 33 BxB, QxP ch.

| 31 | ... | R-Kt1 ch |
| 32 | K-R3 | |

Not 32 K-B3, P-K5 ch; 33 K-B4, R-Kt5 ch; 34 KxP, Q-Q2 ch; 35 K-B6, R-Kt3 mate.

32	...	Q-KKt2!
33	B-Q1	R-K3!
	Resigns	

GAME 55

Besides being so formidable an opponent in the middle-game, Tal is by no means devoid of new ideas in the openings. The following game illustrates his own method of handling the Queen's Indian Defence, the idea being to turn the game not so much onto a combinative track as onto one which poses additional positional problems. As will be seen, these prove too much even for Gligoric.

QUEEN'S INDIAN DEFENCE

	TAL	GLIGORIC
1	P-Q4	Kt-KB3
2	P-QB4	P-K3
3	Kt-KB3	P-QKt3
4	Kt-B3	B-Kt2
5	B-Kt5	

A less well-trodden line than either 5 P-KKt3, or 5 P-K3. After Black's next move the game becomes a Nimzo-Indian and Queen's Indian hybrid.

5	...	B-Kt5
6	P-K3	P-KR3
7	B-R4	P-KKt4

Most of Tal's opponents seem to have chosen this energetic continuation. All the same, a safer line is 7..., BxKt ch; 8 PxB, P-Q3; 9 B-Q3, QKt-Q2; 10 0-0, Q-K2; and then Black can if he likes castle on the Q side and play P-KKt4 and even P-KR4, with still greater effect.

8	B-Kt3	Kt-K5
9	Q-B2	BxKt ch
10	PxB	P-Q3
11	B-Q3	KtxB

In the Tal–Duckstein game, Zurich, 1959 Black tried to reinforce his knight with 11..., P-KB4; but after 12 P-Q5!, PxP; 13 PxP, BxP; 14 Kt-Q4, he was in trouble. In this position Black has to watch out for P-Q5 by White in any case.

12	RPxKt	Kt-Q2
13	P-R4	P-QR4
14	R-QKt1	P-Kt5

It might have been worth playing Q-B3, with a view to 0-0-0, in spite of the open QKt file.

| 15 | Kt-R4 | |

One of the rare cases where a knight is well posted on the edge of the board. It remains there for 24 more moves and then gives the game a decisive turn.

| 15 | ... | Kt-B3 |

16 P–Q5!?

A positional sacrifice of a type often seen in such positions. Should Black take the pawn, White will control his KB5. The question is whether White gets enough for the pawn.

16 ... Q–K2

Since even this does not keep White out of his KB4, PxP at once was better. It is typical of having Tal as an opponent that castling on either side is hazardous.

17	O–O	Kt–Q2
18	PxP	QxP
19	B–B5	QxBP
20	KR–Q1	Kt–B3
21	R–Q4	Q–B3

22 B–K6! R–KKt1

An interesting situation! Clearly 22 ...., PxB; was impossible because of 23 Q–Kt6 ch,

K–Q2; 24 Q–Kt7 ch. But after the text-move White could win the queen by 23 R–QB4, though then Black could obtain counter-play by 23 ..., PxB.

23 B–B4! K–B1

Not 23 ..., O–O–O; 24 BxP, KR–B1; 25 Q–B5 ch, Kt–Q2; 26 R–QB4, thus showing that White's 22nd move was more than a mere bluff, having a useful positional purpose as well.

24	B–Kt5	Q–B4
25	R–QB4	Q–K4
26	RxBP	B–K5
27	B–Q3	P–Q4
28	R–B6	R–Kt1
29	P–QB4!	R–Kt4

Although Black has held his opponent to material equality, his position is less active. Some interesting fighting at close range now follows.

30	P–B5	P–Q5
31	PxQP	QxQP
32	BxB	QxB
33	PxP	QxQ
34	RxQ	Kt–Q2
35	P–Kt7	Kt–B4
36	R–Kt5!	KtxKtP

37 R(B2)–Kt2

Even Homer nods at times! After the cut and thrust of the last few moves Black has found himself able to recover his pawn only at the cost of a grievous pin, which the text-move maintains in spite of the exchange of a pair of rooks. After the exchange, however, the pin has less force and the quick way to win was by 37 Kt–B5!, avoiding the exchange and threatening mate by 38 RxKt, RxR; 39 R–B8. If Black tries 37..., P–B3; against this, White wins by 38 R–B7.

37	...	RxR
38	RxR	K–K2
39	Kt–B5 ch	K–Q2
40	KtxP	K–B2
41	KtxBP	R–KB1
42	Kt–R6	R–Q1
43	R–Kt5	R–Q8 ch
44	K–R2	R–QR8

The position at the adjournment. White still has a win, but it is more difficult now because Black will have a passed QRP.

45	RxKtP	Kt–B4
46	R–QB4	K–B3
47	Kt–B5	RxP
48	Kt–Q4 ch	K–Kt3
49	RxR	KtxR
50	P–Kt4	Kt–B6
51	K–Kt3	P–R5
52	K–B4	P–R6
53	Kt–B2	P–R7
54	P–Kt5	K–B4
55	P–Kt6	Kt–Q4 ch
56	K–Kt5	K–B5
57	P–Kt7	Kt–K2
58	P–B4	

Black is now able to force a Queen end game but it is equally hopeless.

58	...	K–B6
59	Kt–R1	K–Kt7
60	P–B5	KxKt
61	P–B6	K–Kt8
62	PxKt	P–R8=Q
63	P–K8=Q!	Q–R4 ch

Not 63..., QxP ch; 64 Q–Kt6 ch, forcing the queens off. This possibility had to be foreseen by Tal as far back as the 50th move.

| 64 | K–R6 | Resigns |

For 64..., Q–Kt3 or R3 ch; is again met by 65 Q–Kt6 ch, while if 64..., Q–Q7 ch; 65 K–R7, Q–Q6 ch; 66 Q–Kt6, wins.

GAME 56

Against Keres in the 17th round Tal got into an apparently hopeless position but found a problem-like move to ward off the attack. With Keres still trying to win, Tal's energetic counter-play then gave him the advantage. The game is, in fact, a good example of his defensive skill.

SICILIAN DEFENCE

	KERES	TAL
1	P–K4	P–QB4
2	Kt–KB3	P–K3
3	P–Q4	PxP
4	KtxP	P–QR3
5	B–Q3	Kt–QB3
6	KtxKt	QPxKt

Two rounds earlier against Smyslov he played KtPxKt, which is at least as good and the fact that he lost that game had nothing to do with his 6th move. However, with a good lead in the tournament, Tal is not for once particularly anxious to complicate the game.

7	0–0	P–K4
8	Kt–Q2	Q–B2
9	P–QR4	Kt–B3
10	Q–B3	B–QB4
11	Kt–B4	0–0
12	Kt–K3	

Keres still had a chance of winning the tournament if he could defeat Tal now, so he exerts every effort to work up an attack on the king.

12	...	R–K1
13	B–B4	B–K3
14	BxB	RxB
15	Kt–B5	P–KKt3
16	Kt–R6 ch	K–Kt2
17	R–Q1	R–Q1
18	RxR	

18 B–Kt5, was worth considering. White, however, has a far-reaching plan in mind, the point of which is revealed on move 23. Tal has to be very careful.

18	...	QxR
19	B–Kt5	Q–Q5
20	P–R4	

Defending the bishop against the threat of 20..., QxP ch; 21 QxQ, BxQ ch; 22 KxB, KtxP ch. Now White in turn is threatening 21 R–Q1, and if 20..., R–Q3; 21 P–B3, Q–B5; 22 K–R2, and 23 R–Q1, is very strong.

20	...	QxKtP
21	R–Q1	B–Q5
22	R–Q3	

Threatening to force his way in with 23 P–B3, and 24 R–Q7. What is Black to do? If 22..., P–B4; 23 R–Kt3, Q–R8 ch; 24 K–R2, P–KKt3; 25 P–B3, P–B5; 26 R–Kt4, QxBP; 27 QxQ, BxQ; 28 RxBP, and Black might as well resign. So there is nothing to be lost by adopting a bold course.

22	...	QxP
23	RxB	PxR
24	P–K5	

Black is apparently lost, but he finds a fine defensive move.

| 24 | ... | K–B1! |
| 25 | PxKt | |

25 BxKt, is not good for after 25.... Q–B8 ch; 26 K–R2, QxKt; 27 B–Kt5, Q–Kt2; 28 B–B6, RxB; 29 PxR, Q–R3; 30 Q–K4, K–Kt1; 31 QxQP, Q–B1; Black has a winning ending. White could perhaps have got a slightly better game than he did by 25 K–R2, Q–K5; 26 Q–R3 ch, K–K1; 27 PxKt.

| 25 | ... | Q–B6! |

Very strong! He forces the white queen onto an awkward square and wins a pawn into the bargain.

26	Q–Kt4	Q–K8 ch
27	K–R2	QxP
28	Q–R3	Q–K8
29	Q–QKt3	P–Kt4
30	PxP	BPxP
31	Q–R3 ch	P–Kt5
32	Q–QKt3	Q–K4 ch
33	K–R1	Q–K8 ch
34	K–R2	Q–K4 ch

Gaining time on his clock. White cannot play 35 K–R3, because of Q–K6 ch!

| 35 | K–R1 | Q–Q3 |
| 36 | K–Kt1 | |

36 ...   P–Q6

There were better winning chances either
by 36 ..., Q–B4; or by 36 ..., P–R4.
After the text-move White could have
drawn by 37 Q–B4, P–Q7; 38 BxP, QxB;
39 Q–B8 ch, R–K1; 40 Q–B5 ch. Even if
Black answered 37 Q–B4, with 37 ....
P–R4; White could hardly lose after
38 Q–B8 ch, R–K1; 39 Q–B4. However,
Keres missed this saving line in extreme
time trouble.

37	Q–Q1?	Q–B4 ch
38	K–R1	Q–QB7
39	Q–B3	P–Q7
40	BxP	QxB
	Resigns	

GAME 57

The Tal–Olafsson game is an alternation
of brightness and shadow, like the light
from a flawed diamond. Tal shows himself an excellent strategist but, unlike his
usual self, he fails to find the tactical solution in a strategically well constructed
position. Olafsson thus gained an advantage but blundering more than once in
time trouble he allowed Tal to gain the
upper hand after all.

RUY LOPEZ

	TAL	OLAFSSON
1	P–K4	P–K4
2	Kt–KB3	Kt–QB3

3	B–Kt5	P–QR3
4	B–R4	Kt–B3
5	O–O	B–K2
6	R–K1	P–QKt4
7	B–Kt3	O–O
8	P–B3	P–Q3
9	P–KR3	Kt–Q2
10	P–Q4	Kt–Kt3
11	QKt–Q2	

In previous games Tal successfully played
11 B–K3. The text-move was used against
him by Spassky at the Soviet Chess Spar-
takiad.

11 ...   PxP

This and the next move form a regular
system of defence. However, B–B3 is also
playable.

12	PxP	P–Q4
13	B–B2!	

Spassky's strong continuation, and much
better than 13 P–K5, B–B4.

13 ...   B–K3

In a game Vasiukov–Furman from a Moscow–Leningrad team match Black played
15 ..., Kt–Kt5; and White got the advantage after 14 B–Kt1, PxP; 15 BxP.
Olafsson follows Tal's own recipe, which
he employed against Spassky.

14	P–K5	Q–Q2
15	Kt–Kt3	

Preparing a plan to occupy the weak QB5,
which he consistently follows.

15 ...   Kt–R5

In the Spassky–Tal game the continuation
was 15 ..., B–KB4; 16 B–Kt5, B–QKt5;
17 R–K2, KR–K1; with adequate play for
Black.

16 B–Kt5 !

20 B–R7 ch?

With the idea of weakening Black's QB4 still further by exchanging the bishop.

16 ... Kt–Kt5?

Not a good idea. Admittedly White would get the advantage after 16..., KtxKtP; by 17 BxP ch, KxB; 18 Q–Kt1 ch, or even by 17 Q–Kt1!, at once. However, Black could get a satisfactory game by 16..., P–B3; 17 PxP, BxP; 18 BxB, RxB. He could also try to keep his bishop by 16..., B–QKt5; 17 R–K2, KR–K1.

17 BxB QxB
18 Q–Kt1 P–R3

If 18..., KtxB; White controls his QB by 19 QxKt, and 20 QR–B1. But 18..., P–Kt3; was a better defence to White's attack.

19 R–QB1 !

Simple and logical. A position that looks most unlike Tal, but a rapid change is in prospect.

19 ... QR–B1

Transposing moves and so robbing himself of the fruits of his previous excellent strategy. Correct was 20 Kt–B5!, KtxKt; 21 B–R7 ch, K–R1; 22 RxKt, P–Kt3; 23 P–R3!, B–B4; 24 Q–QB1, followed either by 24..., Kt–Q6; 25 QxP, or by 24..., KxB; 25 PxKt, with advantage to White in either case. It is rare for Tal to miss a combinative solution of that kind! Now the game is jolted right out of its logical course.

20 ... K–R1
21 Kt–B5

Equally unconvincing is 21 P–R3, P–Kt3; 22 BxP, PxB; 23 QxP, RxKt; 24 QxP ch, Q–R2; or again 21 P–R3, P–Kt3; 22 PxKt, B–B4; 23 Q–R2, QxKtP.

21 ... P–Kt3!

The difference is that Q–B1 is no longer possible.

22 BxP KtxKt
23 RxKt PxB
24 QxP

24 P–R3, is met by 24..., B–B4.

24 ... R–B2?

Much stronger was 24 . . . , B–B4; 25 QxP ch, Q–R2; 26 QxQ ch, BxQ; 27 P–R3, Kt–Q6; 28 R–B6, B–K5.

| 25 | QxP ch | R–R2 |
| 26 | Q–B6 ch | |

If he avoids the exchange of queens, Black will work up a strong attack on his king along the open files.

| 26 | . . . | QxQ |
| 27 | PxQ | Kt–Q6? |

An inaccuracy in severe time trouble. After 27 . . . , R–KKt1; 28 P–R3, Kt–Q6; 29 R–B6, B–B1; White's chances are almost negligible. Is one to say that Tal was lucky again? Only in so far as he has a style that wears out his opponents so that they come to the most critical parts of the game in a state not far short of collapse.

28	R–B6	B–Q2
29	RxRP	R–KKt1
30	P–KR4	Kt–B5?

A decisive mistake in great time trouble. He could get a pull by 30 . . . , B–Kt5!: whether White answered 31 Kt–K5, KtxKt; 32 PxKt, B–B6!; or 31 Kt–Kt5, RxP.

31	P–KKt3	Kt–R6 ch
32	K–Kt2	B–Kt5
33	Kt–K5	Kt–B5 ch
34	K–R2	B–K3?

Black's last two faulty moves show how successfully Tal has infused tension into the position.

| 35 | R–K1 | |

Now he recovers the piece and the win is simple.

35	. . .	B–B4
36	P–B7	R–KB1
37	PxKt	RxP ch
38	K–Kt3	R–R6 ch
39	K–Kt2	K–Kt2

40	R–K3	R–R4
41	R–Kt3 ch	K–R2
42	R–Kt5	Resigns

GAME 58

Tal's next game is another against Fischer, which should delight the reader. He launches a furious attack on Black's king on the 19th move, sacrificing three pawns and a knight. Like so many of Tal's games, this one is valuable for its contribution to opening theory.

KING'S INDIAN DEFENCE

	TAL	FISCHER
1	P–Q4	Kt–KB3
2	P–QB4	P–KKt3
3	Kt–QB3	B–Kt2
4	P–K4	P–Q3
5	B–K2	0–0
6	Kt–B3	P–K4
7	P–Q5	QKt–Q2
8	B–Kt5	

This form of development was introduced by Petrosian. It deviates from the normal line in that 7 . . . , Kt–B3; is prevented, whereas it can follow the usual 7 0–0. Moreover, by not castling on the 8th move either, White does not allow the well-known variations beginning with 8 0–0, Kt–B4. Black is thus faced with less common problems and must act quickly against the threat of 9 Q–Q2.

| 8 | . . . | P–KR3 |
| 9 | B–R4 | P–R3 |

Preventing Kt–QKt5 before playing his next move, but the idea proves to be too cumbersome and slow. Trifunovic recommends 9 . . . , P–KKt4; 10 B–Kt3, Kt–R4; but it is not certain that this is satisfactory since it was given a trial in the Smyslov-Benkő game and White had a pull after

11 0-0, Kt–B5; 12 Kt–Q2, P–KB4; 13 PxP,
KtxB ch; 14 QxKt, Kt–B3; 15 P–B5.

10	0-0	Q–K1
11	Kt–Q2	Kt–R2
12	P–QKt4	B–E3

In the 6th round Fischer played 12 . . . ,
Kt–Kt4; and White was able to carry out
his strategical aim of a Q-side attack by
13 P–B3, P–KB4; 14 B–B2, Q–K2; 15 R–B1,
Kt–B3; 16 P–B5, B–Q2; 17 Q–B2, Kt–R4;
18 P–Kt5! The text-move works out no
better, nor would 12 . . . , P–KB4; 13 PxP,
PxP; 14 B–R5.

13	BxB	Kt(R2)xB
14	Kt–Kt3	Q–K2
15	Q–Q2	K–R2
16	Q–K3	Kt–KKt1

Although he at last achieves P–KB4, he
loses so much ground in development that
White is able to exploit the position.

17	P–B5	P–B4
18	KPxP	KtPxP

19 P–B4!

Introducing a typical Tal series of sacri-
fices in order to storm the king's position.
Black could try and keep the game closed
by 19 . . . , P–K5; but that would give
White access to his Q4, besides leaving
Black with weaknesses on K3 and KB4.

19	. . .	KPxP
20	QxP	PxP

The acceptance of the pawn offer is fatal.
His only chance was 20 . . . , Q–K4.

21	B–Q3!	PxP
22	QR–K1	Q–B3

23 R–K6!

Much stronger than 23 QxKtP, after which
23 . . . , Kt–K4; would hold the KBP. Now
the attack on the black king develops apace.

23	. . .	QxKt

If 23 . . . , Q–B2; 24 QxKtP, and Black
cannot play Kt–K4.

24	BxP ch	RxB

If 24 . . . , K–R1; 25 RxP ch, wins.

25	QxR ch	K–R1
26	R–B3!	Q–Kt7
27	R–K8!	

Every move is a threat. Black is now faced
with RxKt ch, so he returns the piece.

27	. . .	Kt–B3
28	QxKt ch	QxQ
29	RxQ	K–Kt2
30	R(B6)–B8	Kt–K2

Temporarily avoiding the loss of a piece,
but White's subsequent knight manoeuvre
is decisive.

31	Kt–R5	P–R4
32	P–KR4	R–Kt1
33	Kt–B4	P–Kt4
34	Kt–K5	Resigns

GAME 59

It was said of Lasker that though he sometimes lost a game or two, he never lost his head. The following game shows that Tal possesses the same capacity. He takes too great a risk in the opening and gets into a lost position. However, he continues to defend himself with impressive calm and finally it is his opponent who loses his head and with it the game.

SICILIAN DEFENCE

	FISCHER	TAL
1	P–K4	P–QB4
2	Kt–KB3	P–Q3
3	P–Q4	PxP
4	KtxP	Kt–KB3
5	Kt–QB3	P–QR3
6	B–QB4	P–K3
7	B–Kt3	P–QKt4!?

In the 13th round against the same opponent Tal played the more prudent B–K2. However, it is by no means uncommon for a player to depart from a well-tried line for fear of meeting a prepared variation.

8   P–B4!

The most energetic continuation, whereby he gets ample compensation in development for the sacrifice of a pawn. Tal, quite logically, accepts the offer, though to do so is extremely risky.

8	...	P–Kt5
9	Kt–R4	KtxP
10	O–O!	P–Kt3

As a means of preventing White's P–B5 this turns out quite useless.

11	P–B5	KtPxP
12	KtxBP!	R–Kt1

Not 12..., PxKt; 13 Q–Q5!, R–R2; 14 Q–Q4!, and White wins a rook.

13   B–Q5!

Another excellent move, but though White thus emphasises the superiority of his position, Tal defends himself with the utmost coolness and contrives to put every possible difficulty in his opponent's way.

13	...	R–R2
14	BxKt	PxKt
15	BxP	R–K2
16	BxB	QxB
17	B–B4?	

Overlooking that the simple 17 P–B3, maintained his advantage because of the mating threats that follow and even if Black succeeds in surviving to the end-game, he would still have the weaker pawns. Nevertheless, White's game is by no means ruined by this slip.

17	...	Q–B3
18	Q–B3	QxKt
19	BxP	Q–B3
20	BxKt	Q–Kt3 ch
21	K–R1	QxB

22 Q–B6 ch?

But this is a grave error. He had good chances by 22 QR–K1!, since then the threats of 23 Q–B6 ch, and 23 QxP ch, are not easy to meet.

22	...	R–Q2
23	QR–K1 ch	B–K2
24	RxP	KxR
25	Q–K6 ch	K–B1
26	QxR	Q–Q3
27	Q–Kt7	R–Kt3
28	P–B3	P–QR4
29	Q–B8 ch	K–Kt2
30	Q–B4	B–Q1
31	PxP	PxP
32	P–KKt3?	

As long as the queens remained on the board there were drawing chances for White, and therefore 32 P–QR3, was preferable. Now Black is able to exchange the queens and come out with a certain win.

32	...	Q–B3 ch
33	R–K4	QxQ
34	RxQ	R–Kt3
35	K–Kt2	K–B3
36	K–B3	K–K4
37	K–K3	B–Kt4 ch
38	K–K2	K–Q4
39	K–Q3	B–B3
40	R–B2	B–K4
41	R–K2	R–KB3
42	R–QB2	R–B6 ch
43	K–K2	R–B2
44	K–Q3	B–Q5
45	P–QR3	P–Kt6
46	R–B8	BxP
47	R–Q8 ch	K–B3
48	R–QKt8	R–B6 ch
49	K–B4	R–B6 ch
50	K–Kt4	K–B2
51	R–Kt3	B–R8
52	P–QR4	P–Kt7
	Resigns	

MIKHAIL TAL, THE NEW WORLD CHESS CHAMPION

The struggle between Botvinnik and Tal in the large auditorium of the Pushkin Theatre in Moscow during the spring of 1960 was watched with absorbed and passionate interest. This interest derived not only from the occasion itself but from the clash of styles involved, and especially the style of the younger Mikhail, whose fighting qualities and brilliant imagination were already such a byword; hundreds of thousands of chess-players throughout the world followed the drama as it unfolded. The excitement reached its peak at the end of the 21st game of the match, when Tal was literally carried shoulder-high from the arena. As an incident that final wave of enthusiasm may have been of little importance, but it was symptomatic of an advance in the art of chess and in the popularity of the game which can be ascribed directly to Tal's success.

Tal went off with a rush and took the lead in the first game. Though a number of draws came later, Tal continued his advance and Botvinnik was only momentarily to apply the brakes. The final decision was virtually reached in the 19th game, when Botvinnik's resistance was finally broken and the challenger had merely to score two more draws to win the title.

The match revealed Tal for the most part as an expert in positional manoeuvres, although he was seen in his old colours in the first and sixth games; indeed, in the latter it could be said that even more delicate and refined colours came from his palette. Even since the recent Candidates' tournament his outlook on chess had matured and in the course of the match itself the process continued.

His own words after his win are worth recording: "Admittedly the match was no easy one, and to win it less so. Analysis of adjourned positions caused me and my second, A. Koblentz, to burn a great deal of midnight oil. I was naturally delighted at the opportunity of engaging so fine a master as Botvinnik and our meeting undoubtedly produced play of the highest standard.

"How did I prepare for the match? Well, I can reveal that secret now. I gave little attention to the openings since I regarded them as of minor importance. What I tried to do was to detect Botvinnik's vulnerable points from a study of his games; further, I studied much chess literature and got to know the achievements of Soviet and other masters. My preparation goes right back to the Riga tournament, where I studied openings more than anything else. I engaged in no match-play at all so as to have all the more appetite for it when it came.

"I took very little time over he openings in almost every game with Botvinnik so as to come to the later part of the game as fresh as possible."

In Tal's opinion Botvinnik's play in the 10th game was that of a true virtuoso. Of his own wins he thought the 19th game was the best. All the same, the 12th game is notable with its extreme wealth of ideas.

GAME 60

The first game with Botvinnik can be called the fulfilment of a dream. Tal had always wanted to play a game with the world champion. Now his opportunity had come, not to play a single game but a whole match. But there was nothing dream-like in his play, which shows him attacking vigorously and overwhelming Botvinnik with his energy, thus securing a lead in the match which he never lost.

FRENCH DEFENCE

	TAL	BOTVINNIK
1	P–K4	P–K3
2	P–Q4	P–Q4
3	Kt–QB3	

Selecting the variation which leads to the sharpest complications.

3	...	B–Kt5

Botvinnik always plays this move, which has quite superseded the older Kt–KB3 or PxP.

4	P–K5	P–QB4
5	P–QR3	

Russian analysis has shown this to give White most chances and Bogolyubov's B–Q2 is now rarely seen.

5	...	BxKt ch
6	PxB	Q–B2

The alternative is 6 ..., Kt–K2; so as to defend the KKtP after 7 Q–Kt4, by 7 ..., Kt–B4.

7	Q–Kt4	P–B4
8	Q–Kt3	Kt–K2

Black has to choose between this move and PxP. The latter move was played by Botvinnik against Reshevsky in Moscow in 1948 and by Fuchs against Spassky at Varna in 1958, but *Chess Archives* concluded that Black did not get a satisfactory game, though that is an opinion which could easily change. The text-move was played by Petrosian against Gligoric at the Candidates' tournament of 1959.

9	QxP	R–Kt1
10	QxP	PxP

11	K–Q1

Petrosian's appraisal of the position was the following: "The threat of a storm hangs over the black king, for the white queen has gone deep into his position and opened it up by the removal of the KKtP and the KRP. Still, Black has now started a good counter-attack on the QB file and White has to guard against both QxBP ch and QxKP ch. The move selected is more promising than the alternative 11 K–K2." It is amusing to recall that a few months earlier Botvinnik, when visiting Nürnberg, saw the castle, so impregnable in the Middle Ages, surrounded by its moat and remarked: "That's the sort of place to withdraw to when Tal is on the attack."

11	...	B–Q2

No doubt both players had had a good look at the previously mentioned game between Gligoric and Petrosian, where Gligoric similarly surprised his opponent with 11 K–Q1. Petrosian gave the situation half an hour's thought, played 11 ..., QKt–B3; and was soon in a lost position although he later escaped with a draw. Botvinnik's alternative selection requires more practical tests before its true value can be assessed.

12	Q–R5 ch	Kt–Kt3

Petrosian preferred K–Q1 here.

13	Kt–K2	P–Q6

Trying to accelerate his counter-chances against the threat of Kt–B4. An interesting idea is raised by the following Yugoslav analysis: 13 ..., PxP; 14 Kt–B4, K–B2; 15 Q–R7 ch, R–Kt2; 16 Q–R6, QxP; 17 Kt–R5, Kt–B3; 18 QxR ch, QxQ; 19 KtxQ, KxKt; 20 P–B4, preventing P–K4 and P–Q5. It is difficult to assess the value of this line as it is to appraise the game itself.

14	PxP	B–R5 ch
15	K–K1	QxP?

It was better to move the king to safety with Kt–B3 and o–o–o, though he would still have had difficulty in getting compensation for his two lost pawns.

16	B–Kt5!	Kt–B3
17	P–Q4	Q–B2
18	P–R4	P–K4?

This was his last chance of getting the king to safety by Kt–K2 and o–o–o. If White answers 18 ..., Kt–K2; with 19 BxKt, then 19 ..., QxB; 20 Kt–B4, Q–KB2; 21 KtxKt,

RxKt; and Black still has some powers of resistance. As it is, the king is caught in the centre and plagued with attack on all sides.

19	R–R3!	

An excellent move. The rook is developed, his QB3 is defended and Black's Kt–K2 is now able to be answered with PxP.

19	...	Q–B2
20	PxP	Kt(B3)xP
21	R–K3	K–Q2

An attempt to win the queen by 21 ..., R–R1; is illusory, for then comes 22 RxKt ch, K–Q2; 23 R–K7 ch, QxR; 24 QxKt.

22	R–Kt1!	P–Kt3

22 ..., B–B3; 23 Kt–Q4, does not promise much more.

23	Kt–B4	QR–K1
24	R–Kt4	

The white rooks enter the action in most original fashion.

24	...	B–B3
25	Q–Q1!	KtxKt
26	R(Kt4)xKt	Kt–Kt3
27	R–Q4	RxR ch
28	PxR	K–B2

29	P–B4!	

From the 22nd move White has been re-grouping his forces for an attack on Black's

Q4, and now the decisive break-through occurs. Black's reply is an error in time trouble but other moves would also have led to loss of the QP and ultimately of the game.

29	. . .	PxP?
30	BxP	Q–Kt2
31	BxR	QxB
32	P–R5	Resigns

GAME 61

This game is as much a pearl as the famous 6th game of the return match between Alekhine and Euwe. Sacrifices like Black's 21 . . . , Kt–B5; cannot be evaluated in the time available for play, and even Botvinnik failed to disprove it. Certainly Tal's win in this game was an important factor in the battle of nerves, while his combinative ability is revealed at its best.

KING'S INDIAN DEFENCE

	BOTVINNIK	TAL
1	P–QB4	Kt–KB3
2	Kt–KB3	P–KKt3
3	P–KKt3	B–Kt2
4	B–Kt2	O–O
5	P–Q4	P–Q3
6	Kt–B3	QKt–Q2
7	O–O	P–K4
8	P–K4	P–B3
9	P–KR3	Q–Kt3

This move, with an eye to the squares Q5 and QKt7, certainly sets White as many problems as Q–R4. White's problem really is to defend the two attacked squares and at the same time retain an initiative; besides the text-move, four other moves come into consideration for White, viz.:

I. 10 R–K1, maintaining the tension, is probably the best, for after 10 . . ., PxP; 11 KtxP, Kt–Kt5; White does not have to take the knight but can play 12 Kt(B3)–K2, when

Black's initiative is shown to be quite ephemeral by 12 . . ., Kt(Kt5)–K4; 13 P–Kt3, Kt–B4; 14 B–K3, Kt(K4)–Q6; 15 R–KB1.

II. 10 R–Kt1, although similarly maintaining tension, is not favourable because of 10 . . ., PxP; and if 11 KtxP, KtxP; or 11 QxP, Kt–B4.

III. 10 P–B5, is too sharp. For example, 10 . . ., PxBP; 11 PxKP, Kt–K1.

IV. 10 PxP, giving equal chances as in Najdorf–Bronstein in Moscow in 1956, which went 10 . . ., PxP; 11 Q–K2 (defending his QKtP), Kt–K1; 12 B–K3, Q–Kt5; 13 P–B5!. P–Kt3!

| | 10 | P–Q5 | PxP! |

In the Geller–Wade game at Stockholm, 1952, Black was quickly at a disadvantage after 10 . . ., Kt–K1?; 11 R–Kt1, P–KB4; 12 Kt–KKt5

| 11 | BPxP | Kt–B4 |
| 12 | Kt–K1 | |

The alternative is 12 Q–B2, B–Q2; 13 B–K3, as in the game Korchnoi–Nejmetdinov, 1957, though Spassky and Tolush, analysing that game, considered 13 . . ., P–QR4! satisfactory to Black.

12	. . .	B–Q2
13	Kt–Q3	KtxKt
14	QxKt	

| 14 | . . . | KR–B1! |

An unexpected move which reveals Tal's profound position judgement and his freedom from dogma. One is reminded of a game between Lasker and Janowsky, where Lasker, with equally profound insight, played his rook to an unexpected square, where it was later found to have a very good post.

| 15 | R–Kt1 | Kt–R4! |
| 16 | B–K3 | Q–Kt5 |

Now 17 . . . , P–B4; is threatened and if 17 P–R3, Q–Kt6.

17 Q–K2

So that after 17 . . . , P–B4; 18 PxP, Black cannot play 18 . . . , PxP.

17	. . .	R–B5
18	KR–B1	QR–QB1
19	K–R2	P–B4
20	PxP	BxP
21	R–QR1	

Expecting the threat of P–Kt4 to force the retirement of one of the black minor pieces, after which he can prepare to occupy his K4, but a great surprise follows.

21 . . .   Kt–B5!?

A beautiful and by no means unreasonable sacrifice, for though White could reach a better position than he did, such a line is not easy to find among the many possibilities opened up by a move of this nature.

| 22 | PxKt | PxP |
| 23 | B–Q2 | QxP |

Petrosian was of the opinion that Black gave up his advantage by this move and should have played B–K4, with the continuation 24 K–Kt1, QxP; 25 QR–Kt1, BxR; 26 RxB, Q–B7; 27 R–QB1, Q–B4; or else 24 B–B3, QxP; 25 Kt–Q1!, Q–R6!; 26 RxR, RxR; when 27 QxR, is answered by QxB. But in the latter variation the substitution of 24 P–B3, for 24 B–B3, prevents QxB, and then the variation is no longer favourable to Black.

24 QR–Kt1

A line worth considering was 24 Kt–Q1, Q–K4; 25 QxQ, BxQ; 26 B–KB3!, with advantage to White, though actually Tal would have met 24 Kt–Q1, with QxQR!; involving enormous complications.

| 24 | . . . | P–B6! |
| 25 | RxQ? | |

This is the decisive mistake. The correct move was 25 BxP!, BxR; 26 RxB, Q–B7; 27 R–QB1! (not 27 RxP, BxKt; 28 Q–K6 ch, K–R1; 29 Q–K7, B–K4 ch; 30 K–Kt2, R(B5)–B2; 31 RxR, QxR; and Black wins), Q–Kt7; and now White could virtually force a draw by 28 R–QKt1, or even play for a win by 28 B–Kt4.

25	. . .	PxQ
26	R–Kt3	R–Q5!
27	B–K1	B–K4 ch
28	K–Kt1	

28 . . .   B–B5

Recovering the piece either by 29 R–R1, RxKt; 30 RxR, R–Q8; or by 29 R(Kt3)–Kt1, QBxR; 30 RxB, RxKt. Quicker, however, and more worthy of Tal was 28 . . . , RxKt!; 29 R(Kt3)xR, R–Q8; 30 R–B7, B–Kt7!; as suggested by Petrosian.

29	KtxP	RxR
30	KtxR(Q4)	RxB ch
31	B–B1	B–K5
32	Kt–K2	B–K4
33	P–B4	B–B3
34	RxP	BxP
35	R–QB7	

Not 35 RxQRP?, RxKt; 36 BxR, B–Q5 ch.

| 35 | . . . | BxP |
| 36 | RxQRP | |

Safe now, because 36 . . . , RxKt; can be answered by 37 R–R8 ch.

36	. . .	B–B5
37	R–R8 ch	K–B2
38	R–R7 ch	K–K3
39	R–R3	P–Q4
40	K–B2	B–R5 ch
41	K–Kt2	K–Q3
42	Kt–Kt3	BxKt
43	BxB	PxB
44	KxB	K–Q4

The passed pawn wins easily as the white king is cut off.

45	R–R7	P–B6
46	R–QB7	K–Q5
	Resigns	

After considering the position during the adjournment.

GAME 62

Botvinnik has frequently played the Caro-Kann Defence in recent years and here, for the sake of attack with a view to scoring a win, he employs the defence more elastically and with a greater degree of risk. Tal, however, soon finds the answer and launches a fierce attack with a whirl of complications. A slip in such positions is all too easy, and especially so against Tal.

CARO-KANN DEFENCE

TAL	BOTVINNIK
1 P–K4	P–QB3
2 P–Q4	P–Q4
3 Kt–QB3	PxP
4 KtxP	B–B4
5 Kt–Kt3	B–Kt3
6 KKt–K2	Kt–Q2

More active than P–K3, as played in the fifth game. Once White has played his KKt to K2 instead of B3, Black is generally well advised to seek counter-play by P–K4 and the text-move prepares for this.

7 P–KR4	P–KR3
8 Kt–B4	B–R2
9 B–B4	P–K4
10 Q–K2	Q–K2
11 PxP	QxKP
12 B–K3	B–QB4
13 BxB	

White cannot avoid the exchange of queens, for if 13 0–0–0, then BxB; 14 PxB, KKt–B3; and Black completes his development in comfort while White is saddled with a weak KP.

13	. . .	QxQ ch
14	KxQ	KtxB
15	KR–K1	Kt–B3
16	P–Kt4	QKt–Q2
17	K–B1 dis. ch	

Tal has been able to indulge in tactical play even with the queens off and as a result he now succeeds in delaying the development of Black's KR. However, he has achieved this only at the cost of weakening the Q-side pawns and it is only now that the struggle starts in earnest.

17	...	K–B1
18	B–Kt3	P–KKt4
19	PxP	PxP
20	Kt–R3	R–KKt1
21	KR–Q1	

A move that shows he is still looking for an initiative by getting counter-play on the Q file. He could have saved a tempo by QR–Q1, but then Black would achieve further exchanges by 21..., R–K1.

21	...	P–R4
22	PxP	RxP
23	R–Q6	K–K2
24	QR–Q1	R–K4

Played after long consideration, and yet Kt–B4 held out more chance of play against White's weak Q side. He may have feared 24..., Kt–B4; 25 R(Q6)–Q2, KtxB; 26 R–K1 ch, but after 26..., K–B1; the defence of White's Q side is still not easy. Now Tal has the chance of complicating the game.

| 25 | Kt–R5 | B–Kt3? |

And already Black overlooks a simple threat, which could quite well have been disposed of by R–K1 or B–B4.

26	RxKt ch!	KtxR
27	RxKt ch	KxR
28	Kt–B6 ch	K–Q3
29	KtxR	R–QB4
30	Kt–R6	P–B3
31	Kt–Kt4	BxP?

This plan turns out to be faulty. He should retain his K-side pawns and his bishop, because as played the white K-side pawns get too clear a run.

32	KtxBP	BxB?
33	PxB	R–Kt4
34	KtxP	RxP
35	P–B4	

Black cannot stop this pawn, while his own pawns are too slow getting under way.

35	...	R–Kt8 ch
36	K–B2	R–Kt7 ch
37	K–B3	R–Kt6 ch
38	K–Kt4	R–Kt7
39	P–Kt3	P–Kt4
40	Kt(B6)–K4 ch	K–Q4
41	P–B5	P–Kt5
42	P–B6	R–QR7
43	P–B7	R–R1
44	Kt–R7	P–Kt6

If KxKt; 45 Kt–B6 ch, and 46 Kt–K8.

45	Kt–Q2	P–Kt7
46	K–B3!	K–Q5
47	K–K2	P–B4
48	P–B8=Q	RxQ
49	KtxR	P–B5
50	Kt–K6 ch	K–Q4

Or K–B6; 51 P–Kt4.

| 51 | Kt–B4 ch | K–Q5 |
| 52 | Kt–Kt1 | Resigns |

GAME 63

Having failed to gain much advantage against the Caro-Kann Defence, Tal experiments with a kind of Réti opening. Not that he despairs of 1 P–K4, but probably he had no innovation up his sleeve at the moment. Even in the more solid opening selected here Tal found the opportunity for a pawn sacrifice, which Botvinnik declined. This led to a quick development of White's attack, and the bishop sacrifice on the 46th move reminds us that not all gold has to glitter.

RÉTI OPENING

	TAL	BOTVINNIK
1	Kt–KB₃	Kt–KB₃
2	P–KKt₃	P–KKt₃
3	B–Kt₂	B–Kt₂
4	o–o	o–o
5	P–B₄	P–B₃
6	P–Kt₃	Kt–K₅
7	P–Q₄	P–Q₄

Reaching a position similar to certain variations of the Grunfeld Defence. The frontiers between modern openings are often ill-defined. Black's counter-play is aimed at White's QB4 and in three more moves interesting developments arise.

8	B–Kt₂	B–K₃
9	QKt–Q₂	

9	...	KtxKt
10	QxKt!	

A true Tal move. 10..., PxP; accepting the pawn offer, would lead to incalculable complications after 11 Kt–Kt5, PxP; 12 KtxB, PxKt; 13 PxP, Q–Kt3; 14 Q–K3! Tal would then be in his element and Botvinnik can hardly be blamed for refusing the offer.

10	...	Kt–R₃

A more accurate development was P–KR3 followed by Kt–Q2 so as to keep control of his K4.

11	QR–B₁	Q–Q₃
12	Kt–K₅	KR–Q₁
13	KR–Q₁	QR–B₁
14	Q–R₅!	

Preparing an attack on Black's centre by P–K4. Hence Black's decision to simplify by exchanges.

14	...	PxP
15	KtxP	Q–B₂
16	Q–K₁!	

Capablanca would probably have exchanged queens in the expectation of a favourable end-game. But dynamic players like Tal and Alekhine, who have great combinative strength and prefer the middle-game with all its complications, always follow the principle that if the opponent is hard pressed, exchanges should be avoided in order to prevent any easing of the problems of defence.

16	...	Q–Kt₁

Making room for the knight.

17	P–K₄	BxKt
18	RxB	

Not 18 PxB, P–QB4! Now if 18.... P–QB4; 19 P–K5, is strong.

18	...	Kt–B₂
19	B–KR₃	P–K₃

20	B–QB₁!	

Threatening B–B4 and P–Q5, and in any case giving the bishop a more effective diagonal. So Black decides to withdraw his queen.

20 ... Q–R1

Not quite as passive and innocent as it looks at first sight. There is a threat of P–QKt4 (possible now that the queen is defending QB3) with the resulting win of the white QP. White's reply puts paid to that threat.

21 B–Kt5! R–K1

He has nothing better. If R–Q2, there would be a constant threat of P–Q5 by White.

22 Q–Q2 P–KB4
23 B–R6

The only move of Tal's to which exception can be taken. He offers Black the chance of a relieving exchange in direct conflict with the principle outlined in the note to the 16th move above. R–K1 was stronger.

23 .. B×B
24 Q×B R–K2
25 R–K1 R–B1
26 R–B5 Q–Q1!

Botvinnik has defended himself excellently. His 22nd move opened the second rank so that he could defend his king with his major pieces, he has successfully regrouped his forces and by attacking the QP has brought his queen into effective action. Thus the chances have once more become equalized. It is, however, a characteristic of Tal's peculiar talent that he is at once able to find a continuation which again introduces complications and burdens his opponent with the need to solve new problems. This is typical of the "spiteful" nature of his play.

27 R–K5! R–Kt2

Though not a mistake, this is excessively prudent and betrays some psycho-

logical hesitation. By 27 ..., Q×P; 28 P×P, KtP×P; 29 B×P, R(K2)–B2!; 30 R(K5)–K4, Q–B3; Black would have ensured an early draw.

28 Q–Q2 Q–Q3
29 B–B1! R–Q2!
30 P×P R×P
31 R(K5)–K4 R–B3?

Horribly passive! By countering with 31 ..., R–Q4; he would have left White with nothing better than 32 B–B4, leading to multiple exchanges and complete equality. Now Tal assumes direction of the game.

32 P–KR4!

An attack on Black's K3 alone would be insufficient, so he aims to create other weaknesses in Black's game.

32 ... K–Kt2
33 P–R5 P×P
34 R–R4 K–Kt1
35 B–Q3

Like the other bishop earlier, this one now finds greater scope on a new diagonal.

35 ... R–Kt2
36 R–K5 R(B3)–B2
37 Q–R6 Q–K2
38 R(K5)×RP

An interesting position with all the forces, both of attack and defence, except for the knight, directed at Black's KR2. In eight more moves that will in fact prove to be the decisive square, but further regrouping is necessary first and in the meantime Black is very hard pressed.

38	...	Kt–Q4
39	Q–Q2	Kt–B3
40	R–R6	Q–Q3
41	R–B4!	

Black sealed the next move, and subsequent analysis showed that a good defence is hardly to be found.

41	...	Q–B1
42	Q–K3!	Kt–Q4
43	RxR	QxR
44	Q–K5!	

To be satisfied with the win of a pawn by 44 QxP, QxQ; 45 RxQ, would be wrong since Black could then lead into a rook ending by 45 ..., Kt–B5; and White would have great difficulty in forcing a win. Now, however, RxKP is a real threat.

| 44 | ... | Kt–B2 |
| 45 | Q–QB5! | |

Curiously enough, the decision is reached by attacks on the two rook's pawns.

| 45 | ... | Q–B6 |

46 BxP ch!

Like the great painters, Tal too has an eye for an opportunity. Here he sees the main point and employs the piece sacrifice to reach it. Black would have done no better by 45 ..., P–R3; because of 46 Q–Kt6, Kt–Q4; 47 Q–Q8 ch, Q–B1; 48 BxP ch, winning by similar means.

46	...	RxB
47	Q–Kt5 ch	K–R1
48	Q–Q8 ch	K–Kt2
49	RxR ch	KxR
50	QxKt ch	K–Kt3
51	QxKtP	

As a result of his combination he has reached an end-game in which he is two pawns up and which he wins with accurate play.

| 51 | ... | Q–K5 |
| 52 | Q–R6! | |

Not 52 QxRP, Q–K8 ch; 53 K–Kt2, Q–K5 ch; 54 K–R2, Q–K7.

52	...	Q–Kt8 ch
53	K–Kt2	Q–K5 ch
54	K–B1!	Q–Kt8 ch
55	K–K2	Q–B7 ch

Now if Q–K5 ch; 56 K–Q2!, QxP ch; 57 Q–Q3 ch.

56	K–B3	Q–B4 ch
57	K–K3	Q–Kt4 ch
58	K–K2	Q–R4 ch
59	K–Q2	K–B3
60	QxBP	Q–R4 ch
61	Q–B3	QxP ch
62	K–K3	K–B2
63	P–Q5!	

Introducing the final chapter with a temporary pawn sacrifice. He drives the black king back and then, by threatening mate, forces the exchange of queens.

63	...	PxP
64	Q–B7 ch	K–K3
65	Q–B6 ch	K–K2
66	QxP	Q–R8
67	Q–K4 ch	K–B2

68	K-B4!	Q-B8 ch
69	K-Kt4	Q-QR8
70	Q-Q5 ch	K-B1
71	K-B5	Q-Kt8 ch
72	K-B6	Resigns

For after 72 ..., Q-R8 ch; 73 K-K6, White will very soon force the exchange of queens.

GAME 64

With this win Tal breathed freely at last. Botvinnik's resistance was broken and Tal's advantage increased to four points. The remaining draws were little more than a matter of form and it can be safely said that it was after this game that Tal became the new World Champion.

DUTCH DEFENCE

	TAL	BOTVINNIK
1	P-QB4	P-KB4
2	Kt-KB3	Kt-KB3
3	P-KKt3	P-KKt3

This, the Leningrad variation aims at building up positions similar to those in the King's Indian Defence without the loss of a tempo in playing P-KB4. The drawback of the variation is that White is easily able to build up a strong centre. However, other variations of the Dutch Defence, such as the Stonewall, were too likely to lead to a drawn position to suit Botvinnik at this stage. Unfortunately the Leningrad variation proves an unhappy choice also.

4	B-Kt2	B-Kt2
5	P-Q4	P-Q3
6	Kt-B3	P-·K3

Against other moves White could play 7 P-Q5!, and cramp Black horribly. But now, seeing Black with a weak KP, Tal mobilizes P-K4 as soon as he can, then develops threats on the Q side, and not only does he obtain an advantage in space but also the use of open lines.

7	0-0	0-0
8	Q-B2!	

More energetic than either P-Kt3 or R-K1, both of which moves would be answered with 8..., Kt-K5!; equalizing.

8	...	Kt-B3
9	R-Q1	

According to Krogius, 9 P-K4, would be premature on account of 9..., PxP; 10 KtxP, KtxKt; 11 QxKt, P-K4!; with good counter-play. On the other hand, Krogius is of the opinion that 9 P-Q5!, was a good move, to be followed either by 9..., PxP; 10 PxP, Kt-QKt5; 11 Q-Kt3, Kt-R3; 12 B-K3, with B-Q4 to follow, or by 9..., Kt-K4; 10 PxP, KtxP; 11 Kt-QKt5, P-Q4; 12 P-Kt3. The text-move is equally an energetic choice.

9	...	Q-K2

As promising as any other move.

10	R-Kt1	

P-K4 or P-Q5 were equally good, but Tal wants to establish some threats on the Q side at the same time as he breaks open the centre, relying on Black's limited manoeuvring space.

10	...	P-QR4
11	P-QR3	Kt-Q1
12	P-K4!	

143

Tal has solved the problems of the opening in excellent fashion, for he now has a strong centre and an advantage in space, while the harmonious co-ordination of his pieces makes a pleasing impression.

| 12 | ... | PxP |

Rejecting P–K4 because of 13 PxKP, QPxP; 14 B–Kt5, P–B3; 15 P–QKt4, with a positional pull, or even 15 Kt–QR4, with combinative chances.

| 13 | KtxP | KtxKt |
| 14 | QxKt | Kt–B2 |

His only sound plan is to play P–K4, which the knight move prepares for, but 14 . . . , Kt–B3; was preferable for the purpose as it also shields the QKtP.

| 15 | B–R3! |

An unpleasant little move, which shows why 14 . . . , Kt–B3; should have been played. Black can now only play P–K4 at the cost of a pawn by 15 . . . , P–K4; 16 BxB, QRxB; 17 QxKtP, P–K5; 18 Kt–K1.

| 15 | ... | Q–B3 |
| 16 | B–Q2 |

Threatening B–B3 and hustling Black into proceeding with his changed plan.

| 16 | ... | P–Q4 |

Having had to abandon the idea of P–K4, Black finds an alternative which seems to lead to equality.

| 17 | Q–K2 | PxP |

Or 17 . . . , Kt–Q3; 18 Kt–K5, PxP; 19 B–B4. with play similar to that in the actual game.

| 18 | B–B4 | Kt–Q3 |
| 19 | Kt–Kt5 | R–K1 |

An alternative was to counter-attack on the white QP with 19 . . . , Kt–B4; but after

20 QxP, KtxQP; 21 RxKt, QxR; 22 BxP ch, an unclear situation would result but probably with more chances for White than in the line actually chosen.

| 20 | B–Kt2 | R–R3 |
| 21 | Kt–K4! |

Elastically increasing his advantage. First he cramped Black's game, then gradually induced weaknesses of which the most glaring is that on his K3 and now he changes the character of the game again. It is at such moments that the opponent is most likely to commit an error, and such changes are thus an important feature in a fight maintained by psychological means.

21	...	KtxKt
22	BxKt	P–QKt4
23	P–Kt3!	PxP
24	QxP	R–B1
25	QxKtP	R–Kt3
26	Q–K3?

A slight inaccuracy which he will later regret. After 26 Q–B2, RxR; 27 QxR, the win would be easier.

| 26 | ... | RxR |
| 27 | BxR | B–Kt2! |

28	B–R2	B–Q4
29	BxB	PxB
30	BxP	P–R5
31	R–Q3!	

He still has the better game but it is difficult to make use of the extra pawn against the major pieces, Tal accordingly resorts to combinative methods.

31	...	Q–B4
32	B–K5	B–R3
33	Q–K2	R–B1
34	R–KB3!	

A fine move against which there is no defence.

34	...	Q–R6

The alternatives were Q–K5 and R–B7. The first would be answered by 32 Q–R6!, and the second by 32 RxQ, RxQ; 33 R–B6, B–Kt2; 34 R–R6!, BxB; 35 R–K6, with a winning end-game.

35	B–B7!	

The bishop cannot be taken because of mate.

35	...	B–B1

The defence could have been prolonged by 35 ..., Q–Q2; 36 B–R5, Q–R6; 37 B–B3, though Black's king is still faced with the same threats as in the game.

36	Q–Kt5	Q–K3

If now 36 ..., RxB; 37 QxP ch, K–Kt2; 38 Q–K5 ch, and 39 QxR.

37	B–K5	Q–QB3
38	Q–R5	R–R1

38 ..., BxP; 39 Q–R7, would expose Black to a forced mate.

39	Q–Q2	R–B1
40	K–Kt2	Q–Q2
41	P–R4	Resigns

Botvinnik actually sealed 41 ..., Q–Kt5; but the move was never made for he resigned the game before resuming play.

A CATALOGUE OF SELECTED DOVER BOOKS
IN ALL FIELDS OF INTEREST

A CATALOGUE OF SELECTED DOVER BOOKS
IN ALL FIELDS OF INTEREST

THE NOTEBOOKS OF LEONARDO DA VINCI, edited by J.P. Richter. Extracts from manuscripts reveal great genius; on painting, sculpture, anatomy, sciences, geography, etc. Both Italian and English. 186 ms. pages reproduced, plus 500 additional drawings, including studies for Last Supper, Sforza monument, etc. 860pp. 7⅞ x 10¾.   USO 22572-0, 22573-9 Pa., Two vol. set $12.00

ART NOUVEAU DESIGNS IN COLOR, Alphonse Mucha, Maurice Verneuil, Georges Auriol. Full-color reproduction of Combinaisons ornamentales (c. 1900) by Art Nouveau masters. Floral, animal, geometric, interlacings, swashes — borders, frames, spots — all incredibly beautiful. 60 plates, hundreds of designs. 9⅜ x 8¹/₁₆.   22885-1 Pa. $4.00

GRAPHIC WORKS OF ODILON REDON. All great fantastic lithographs, etchings, engravings, drawings, 209 in all. Monsters, Huysmans, still life work, etc. Introduction by Alfred Werner. 209pp. 9⅛ x 12¼.   21996-8 Pa. $6.00

EXOTIC FLORAL PATTERNS IN COLOR, E.-A. Seguy. Incredibly beautiful full-color pochoir work by great French designer of 20's. Complete Bouquets et frondaisons, Suggestions pour étoffes. Richness must be seen to be believed. 40 plates containing 120 patterns. 80pp. 9⅜ x 12¼.   23041-4 Pa. $6.00

SELECTED ETCHINGS OF JAMES A. McN. WHISTLER, James A. McN. Whistler. 149 outstanding etchings by the great American artist, including selections from the Thames set and two Venice sets, the complete French set, and many individual prints. Introduction and explanatory note on each print by Maria Naylor. 157pp. 9⅜ x 12¼.   23194-1 Pa. $5.00

VISUAL ILLUSIONS: THEIR CAUSES, CHARACTERISTICS, AND APPLICATIONS, Matthew Luckiesh. Thorough description, discussion; shape and size, color, motion; natural illusion. Uses in art and industry. 100 illustrations. 252pp.
                                                21530-X Pa. $2.50

TEN BOOKS ON ARCHITECTURE, Vitruvius. The most important book ever written on architecture. Early Roman aesthetics, technology, classical orders, site selection, all other aspects. Stands behind everything since. Morgan translation. 331pp.
                                                20645-9 Pa. $3.50

THE CODEX NUTTALL, A PICTURE MANUSCRIPT FROM ANCIENT MEXICO, as first edited by Zelia Nuttall. Only inexpensive edition, in full color, of a pre-Columbian Mexican (Mixtec) book. 88 color plates show kings, gods, heroes, temples, sacrifices. New explanatory, historical introduction by Arthur G. Miller. 96pp. 11⅜ x 8½.   23168-2 Pa. $7.50

EGYPTIAN MAGIC, E.A. Wallis Budge. Foremost Egyptologist, curator at British Museum, on charms, curses, amulets, doll magic, transformations, control of demons, deific appearances, feats of great magicians. Many texts cited. 19 illustrations. 234pp. USO 22681-6 Pa. $2.50

THE LEYDEN PAPYRUS: AN EGYPTIAN MAGICAL BOOK, edited by F. Ll. Griffith, Herbert Thompson. Egyptian sorcerer's manual contains scores of spells: sex magic of various sorts, occult information, evoking visions, removing evil magic, etc. Transliteration faces translation. 207pp. 22994-7 Pa. $2.50

THE MALLEUS MALEFICARUM OF KRAMER AND SPRENGER, translated, edited by Montague Summers. Full text of most important witchhunter's "Bible," used by both Catholics and Protestants. Theory of witches, manifestations, remedies, etc. Indispensable to serious student. 278pp. 6⅝ x 10. USO 22802-9 Pa. $3.95

LOST CONTINENTS, L. Sprague de Camp. Great science-fiction author, finest, fullest study: Atlantis, Lemuria, Mu, Hyperborea, etc. Lost Tribes, Irish in pre-Columbian America, root races; in history, literature, art, occultism. Necessary to everyone concerned with theme. 17 illustrations. 348pp. 22668-9 Pa. $3.50

THE COMPLETE BOOKS OF CHARLES FORT, Charles Fort. Book of the Damned, Lo!, Wild Talents, New Lands. Greatest compilation of data: celestial appearances, flying saucers, falls of frogs, strange disappearances, inexplicable data not recognized by science. Inexhaustible, painstakingly documented. Do not confuse with modern charlatanry. Introduction by Damon Knight. Total of 1126pp. 23094-5 Clothbd. $15.00

FADS AND FALLACIES IN THE NAME OF SCIENCE, Martin Gardner. Fair, witty appraisal of cranks and quacks of science: Atlantis, Lemuria, flat earth, Velikovsky, orgone energy, Bridey Murphy, medical fads, etc. 373pp. 20394-8 Pa. $3.50

HOAXES, Curtis D. MacDougall. Unbelievably rich account of great hoaxes: Locke's moon hoax, Shakespearean forgeries, Loch Ness monster, Disumbrationist school of art, dozens more; also psychology of hoaxing. 54 illustrations. 338pp. 20465-0 Pa. $3.50

THE GENTLE ART OF MAKING ENEMIES, James A.M. Whistler. Greatest wit of his day deflates Wilde, Ruskin, Swinburne; strikes back at inane critics, exhibitions. Highly readable classic of impressionist revolution by great painter. Introduction by Alfred Werner. 334pp. 21875-9 Pa. $4.00

THE BOOK OF TEA, Kakuzo Okakura. Minor classic of the Orient: entertaining, charming explanation, interpretation of traditional Japanese culture in terms of tea ceremony. Edited by E.F. Bleiler. Total of 94pp. 20070-1 Pa. $1.25

Prices subject to change without notice.
Available at your book dealer or write for free catalogue to Dept. GI, Dover Publications, Inc., 180 Varick St., N.Y., N.Y. 10014. Dover publishes more than 150 books each year on science, elementary and advanced mathematics, biology, music, art, literary history, social sciences and other areas.